nickelodeon

降击神通

AVATAR
THE LAST AIRBENDER™
THE OFFICIAL COOKBOOK

nickelodeon

降击神通

AVATAR

THE LAST AIRBENDER™

THE OFFICIAL COOKBOOK

Recipes From the Four Nations

JENNY DORSEY

INSIGHT
EDITIONS

SAN RAFAEL · LOS ANGELES · LONDON

CONTENTS

AIR NOMADS

WATER TRIBES

EARTH KINGDOM

...CONTINUED

 # THE JASMINE DRAGON TEA SHOP

 # FIRE NATION

AIR NOMADS

In the time since the Hundred Year War, the four nations have been learning how to coexist in peace again, finding ways to connect despite great differences. As the Avatar, I'm pretty good at bringing people together—helping people, it's what I do!—but a hundred years of war have left scars of division on everyone, and it hasn't been easy.

One thing I know for sure is that *everyone* loves to eat (just ask Sokka). To help the four nations come together in harmony and friendship, my friends and I have collected delicious recipes from all over the world. What better way for the nations to learn about each other than through eating?

Food for the Air Nomads was not just about sustenance—it was about having fun with our airbending ingredients and with each other! I'll never forget the good times I had at the Southern Air Temple, where I watched the monks prepare all kinds of treats with expert airbending.

Because so many of our traditions were lost during the Hundred Year War, I've been doing my best to carry on the philosophies of Air Nomad cooking by learning to make dishes I ate as a child and poking around in our archives for recipes I didn't learn to prepare before the war. Sadly, many of the special vegetables and fruits that once grew in abundance among each temple's cloudy peaks are now gone, so I've been re-creating certain items with the best substitutes available in the Earth and Fire nations.

Since I've become such great friends with Katara, Sokka, Zuko, and Toph, I've learned a lot about the foods of their cultures and what they like to eat. No matter the difference in ingredients and flavors, the most important part is always love. As the monks always taught me, you can't construct a tasty meal with ingredients that haven't been properly loved and taken care of. Cooking starts from the seed all the way until the food ends up on our plates.

Many Air Nation foods involve, well, air—so with Toph's (reluctant) help, I've also been revitalizing our stone ovens to bring back some of Monk Gyatso's most famous treats. Practicing airbending for culinary purposes takes time. When baking, make sure you're always checking the strength of your oven's airflow and its temperature for the best cakes and tarts! When steaming, keep the water-and-air circulation steady so your results are tender and evenly done. I can't wait to see what everyone cooks up!

—Aang

MUNG BEAN & TOFU CURRY

Prep Time: 15 minutes
Cook Time: 15 minutes
Yield: Serves 6

Katara says I can't eat Air Nation desserts for every meal, so I've been learning how to make this Mung Bean & Tofu Curry by examining old scrolls I discovered in the Southern Air Temple. After such a long war and so with many temples in shambles, many of these recipes are nearly illegible. With everyone gone, I can't ask for help, so this pressure of legacy rests on me. This version is the closest I've been able to get to the curries I remember. I hope it does my past airbenders justice.

—Aang

2 tablespoons neutral oil

½ yellow onion, peeled and sliced

4 cloves garlic, peeled and minced

1-inch knob fresh ginger, peeled and minced

2 bird's eye chilies, stemmed and minced

1 red bell pepper, stemmed, cored, and sliced

1 green bell pepper, stemmed, cored, and sliced

One 14-ounce block extra firm tofu, drained, pressed, cubed, pan-fried

2 cups cooked green mung beans

2 tablespoons soy sauce, plus more to taste

2 roma tomatoes, diced

1 cup unsalted vegetable stock

2 tablespoons cornstarch

¼ cup chopped cilantro

Heat oil in a large rondeau over medium heat until slick and shiny.

Add onion and sauté 2 to 3 minutes until fragrant.

Add garlic, ginger, and chilies, and sauté 2 to 3 minutes until ginger has softened.

Add red bell pepper, and green bell pepper, and sauté 1 minute.

Add tofu and mung beans with soy sauce, and sauté 3 to 4 minutes.

Add tomatoes and sauté 1 to 2 minutes, or until tomato liquid has been mostly absorbed.

Whisk together vegetable stock with cornstarch until smooth.

Pour mixture into pot and bring to a light boil to activate the starch. The whole gravy should have now thickened considerably.

Mix all ingredients thoroughly to combine, then remove from heat.

Garnish with cilantro.

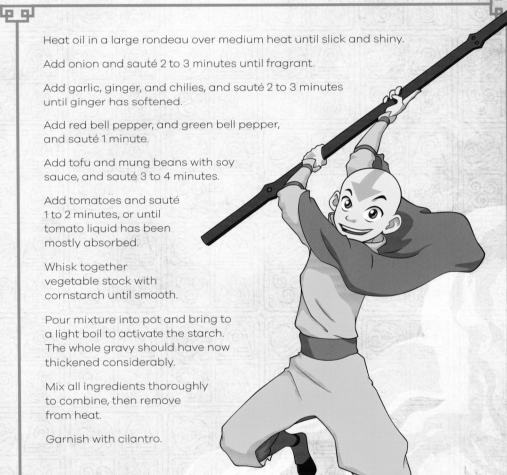

CHRYSANTHEMUM AND SHIITAKE DUMPLINGS

Prep Time:
1 hour

Cook Time:
15 minutes

Yield: About 30 dumplings

Dumplings are a staple when it comes to Air Nation meals. When I was growing up, Monk Gyatso would always surprise me with new filling flavors after tough airbending trainings: cabbage and ginger, chayote and carrot, even sweet ones with milk. (If I'm being honest, they were never *quite* as good as his fruit pies.) This particular flavor has always been one of my favorites; now these are a regular treat I make for Katara and me, though occasionally Momo eats them all before we can!

—Aang

FOR THE DUMPLINGS:

2 tablespoons neutral oil (such as canola or grapeseed), divided

½ medium yellow onion, peeled and sliced

12 shiitake mushroom caps, sliced

Kosher salt

3 cups chrysanthemum greens, tough stalks removed

4 large eggs, beaten until smooth

1 teaspoon cornstarch (optional)

30 round dumpling wrappers of choice

NOTE: Reserve shiitake stems and chrysanthemum stalks and add to the water when steaming or boiling your dumplings!

FOR THE DIPPING SAUCE:

Soy sauce

Rice vinegar

Freshly grated ginger (optional)

Sliced scallions (optional)

TO MAKE THE DUMPLINGS:

Fill a medium pot three-quarters full of water, and bring water to a boil.

In a large sauté pan, heat 1 tablespoon of neutral oil over medium until slick and shiny. Add onion and mushrooms with a dash of salt, and sauté on medium-low to medium until onions have lightly caramelized and mushrooms have reduced significantly, 5 to 8 minutes. Remove from heat and let cool. Reserve.

Once water is boiling, blanch chrysanthemum greens for 30 seconds to 1 minute, or until greens are just barely cooked through. Shock with ice water, and squeeze out all remaining water. Reserve.

In a medium nonstick sauté pan, heat the remaining tablespoon of neutral oil over medium until slick and shiny. Add eggs with a dash of salt, and cook very gently over medium-low heat until completely set on one side, approximately 2 minutes. Flip eggs, and cook gently until second side has set, approximately 2 minutes. Remove eggs from heat, and break up into pieces. Reserve.

Transfer onion, mushrooms, chrysanthemum, and egg to food processor, and pulse until desired consistency. If using, add cornstarch, and pulse again to help bind the filling together. Make sure to scrape the edges of the food processor to incorporate all ingredients.

Once filling is made, set up your dumpling station: a small cutting board to wrap the dumplings, a small bowl of water to wet the wrappers, plus the filling and wrappers themselves.

Wrap dumplings in a shape that makes the most sense for you. The simplest version is to place 2 teaspoons of filling at the center, wet the edges of the wrapper, and fold over to seal in a half-moon shape.

Once formed, dumplings can be cooked by steaming or boiling. Cook until wrappers are translucent and soft. Make sure to use your vegetable scraps in the steaming or boiling water—the Air Nation monks do not approve of wasting food!

TO MAKE THE DIPPING SAUCE:

While dumplings are cooking, mix together soy sauce, rice vinegar, ginger, and scallions in a small bowl to taste. Serve alongside dumplings.

SIMPLE STEAMED VEGETABLES

Prep Time: 15 minutes

Cook Time: 15 minutes

Yield: Serves 2-3

No temple dinner is complete without a plate of steamed vegetables. Through trial and error, I've learned that a mix of root vegetables like taro, potato, or yam; mushrooms like shiitake or oyster; and some watery, crunchy vegetables like bell peppers or tomatoes complete the set. The best part, though, is the dipping sauce! I could probably eat parts of my glider if it were dipped in this sauce . . .

—Aang

FOR THE VEGETABLE DISPLAY:

1 cup peeled, small-diced taro

10 shiitake mushroom caps

10 slices red bell pepper

10 slices yellow bell pepper

10 slices green bell pepper

Kosher salt

FOR THE DIPPING SAUCE:

6 cloves garlic, minced

2-inch knob fresh ginger, peeled and minced

½ cup neutral oil

¼ cup sliced chives

2 tablespoons soy sauce, plus more if needed

2 teaspoons white vinegar, plus more if needed

¼ teaspoon white sugar, plus more if needed

TO MAKE THE VEGETABLES:

Arrange vegetables on the steamer (ideally a steamer that can also be used as the serving platter). Fill steamer pan halfway with water. Cover steamer, and transfer to stovetop.

Bring water to a boil on high heat, then reduce heat to medium. Steam vegetables until tender and cooked through, about 1 minute for the peppers, 5 to 8 minutes for the mushrooms, and 10 minutes for the taro.

TO MAKE THE DIPPING SAUCE:

While vegetables are cooking, combine the garlic and ginger in a heatproof bowl.

In a small pot, heat oil to 350°F, making sure there is least two inches of clearance between the oil and the rim of the pot.

Pour hot oil on top of garlic and ginger. Stir and wait for it to stop foaming. Add chives and stir. Add soy sauce, vinegar, and sugar. Adjust to your liking. Set aside until ready to serve alongside vegetables.

APPA'S APPLE SALAD

Prep Time:
10 minutes

Yield:
Serves 3

Appa is my best friend. He also happens to be a ten-ton flying bison with a big appetite! He loves fresh fruits, veggies, and of course, hay. If we're doing a super long trip and Appa is getting tired, I'll make this salad and airbend it into his haystack as a surprise. The apples give him the energy he needs to keep going. Yip! Yip!

—Aang

½ small red cabbage, cored and sliced thinly (380 grams)

1 Fuji or Gala apple, cored and sliced thinly (220 grams)

2 stalks scallions, stemmed and minced (25 grams)

1-inch knob fresh ginger, peeled and minced (11 grams)

1 teaspoon kosher salt

1½ teaspoon toasted sesame oil

1½ tablespoon rice vinegar

In a medium bowl, combine cabbage, apple, scallions, ginger, salt, sesame oil, and rice vinegar, and mix to combine thoroughly.

Serve.

AANG'S FAVORITE EGG TARTS

Prep Time:
30 minutes (active),
30 minutes (inactive)

Cook Time: 16-20 minutes

Yield: Approximately
6 egg tarts

There is nothing like a freshly baked egg tart. The best ones I've had are from Omashu (don't tell Monk Gyatso!), with a crust made from lychee nuts and a spectacularly smooth and silky custard inside. I heard from Bumi's palace cooks that they learned the ways of the egg tart from Earth Nation merchants after returning home from exploring the world. Maybe one day I can take all of Team Avatar to the land of egg tarts . . . now that would be a dream!

—Aang

FOR THE CRUST:

1 cup all-purpose flour

1 cup toasted barley flour

½ cup hazelnut flour

1 tablespoon toasted white sesame seeds

2 tablespoons cornstarch

1 tablespoon sugar

½ teaspoon kosher salt

¾ cup cold unsalted butter, cubed

3 tablespoons cold water

Cooking spray

FOR THE FILLING:

1 cup unsweetened soy milk

1 tablespoon cornstarch

1 large whole egg plus 2 large egg yolks

⅓ cup white sugar

¼ teaspoon kosher salt

TO MAKE THE CRUST:

Combine the flours, sesame seeds, cornstarch, sugar, and salt in a food processor. Pulse a few times to mix evenly. Add butter, and pulse together until the mixture resembles coarse sand. Add water, a tablespoon at a time, and pulse again until the mixture just comes together. If necessary, add more or less water. Wrap mixture in plastic, and let rest in the refrigerator for 30 minutes.

Unwrap and place mixture between two sheets of parchment paper, and gently roll out until ⅛-inch thick. Let chill in refrigerator until needed. Allow dough to come to just under room temperature before using for molds, so it is more pliable.

TO MAKE THE FILLING:

In a medium pan, whisk together soy milk and cornstarch until smooth.

In a medium bowl, whisk together egg, egg yolks, sugar, and salt until very smooth.

Heat soymilk over medium until just barely bubbling. Carefully temper soy milk into eggs, a quarter cup at a time, and whisk until smooth.

TO ASSEMBLE:

Preheat oven to 400°F. Prepare egg tart molds of choice (3½-inch tart pans will yield approximately six tarts), covering with nonstick spray if needed.

Use a knife or ring cutter to cut dough to fit into egg tart molds. If the crusts break, simply patch them with additional dough.

Pour egg filling into crusts to fill them about three quarters full, using a fine strainer if desired to remove air bubbles. Alternatively, you can blowtorch the bubbles out of the top of the egg tart.

Bake in oven for 10 minutes, then decrease heat to 350°F. Bake for another 10 minutes, or until eggs are firm and cooked through, and cake tester comes out clean. Let rest 5 minutes before removing from molds.

SWEET RICE

I've never met a combination of sweet rice, nuts, and dried berries I didn't like! There are so many flavors and ingredients to experiment with from across the nations, like lychee nuts, dried mangoes, and even ocean kumquats. Katara especially likes a version with cucumberquats, of course. That's why Air Nomads like this recipe—it can be adapted to work with any fruits and nuts no matter where your travels take you!

—Aang

1½ cup uncooked basmati rice

Water, as needed

4 tablespoons unsalted butter, melted

2 tablespoons white sugar

½ teaspoon kosher salt

1½ cup roasted, unsalted cashews

1 cup dried raisins

Combine rice with appropriate amount of water, and cook in rice cooker or on stovetop.

While rice is still hot, combine with butter, sugar, and salt, and mix until thoroughly coated. Add additional sugar or salt if desired.

Add cashews and raisins to rice, stir to combine.

MOMO'S MOON PEACHES

Prep Time: 5 minutes
Cook Time: 5 minutes
Yield: Serves 2-4

There's nothing like a warm moon peach with fresh cream when summer at the Southern Air Temple starts cooling into fall. These are Momo's absolute favorite fruit, so I always keep a good stash handy for him and whip them up whenever we take a trip together to meditate in the wild.

—Aang

2 tablespoons white sugar

1 lemon, zested

¼ cup water

4 donut peaches, stemmed, cored, and chopped (or substitute with any peach variety)

Whipped cream, as desired

Combine sugar, lemon zest, and water in a small pot over medium heat.

Bring mixture to a boil, then remove from heat and let cool 1 minute.

Add chopped peaches. Stir to combine.

Serve sweetened peaches with whipped cream, if desired.

MONK GYATSO'S FRUIT PIES

Prep Time:
30 minutes (active),
1 hour (inactive)

Cook Time:
17-22 minutes

Yield: 4 pies

I don't know if I'll ever be able to make my fruit pies as ooey-gooey as Monk Gyatso's, but I think I'm getting pretty close! The trick to the texture is to really airbend the egg whites until they form fluffy peaks—I like to think of them as sweet replicas of the Kolau Mountains near Omashu. My favorite flavor is purple, but since Monk Gyatso's was always red, I serve them both regularly at the Southern Air Temple. Taking a bite of these special pies always brings back such fond memories of my beloved mentor.

—Aang

FOR THE BASE:

Slightly more than ½ cup white sugar (120 grams)

Slightly more than ½ cup whole milk (150 grams)

¼ cup unsalted butter (60 grams)

Approximately 2½ cups full-fat milk powder (290 grams)

¼ cup roasted pistachios, chopped

FOR THE FILLING:

1½ cups raw cashews, soaked overnight in cold water, drained (yields 280g)

2 lemons, juiced (40 grams)

⅓ cup coconut oil, melted (72 grams)

¾ cup unsweetened milk of choice (160 grams)

⅓ cup maple syrup (100 grams)

½ teaspoon kosher salt

FOR THE TOPPING:

2 large egg whites

½ cup white sugar (100 grams)

¼ teaspoon cream of tartar

TO MAKE THE BASE:

Combine sugar, milk, and butter in a small pot over medium heat.

Stirring constantly, cook until butter and sugar have melted, approximately 2 to 3 minutes.

Reduce heat to low. Add milk powder and continue cooking, stirring continuously until it takes on a dough-like appearance, approximately 5 to 6 minutes. As you stir, it should be able to cleanly pull away from the sides of the pot.

Add pistachios, and cook another 2 to 3 minutes. The mixture should now be able to be shaped with the spatula into a smooth ball.

Scoop an appropriate amount of dough into each silicone mold you're using for the fruit pies, and firmly pat it down with a smooth spatula to create a flat cake base about ¼-inch tall.

Allow base to cool to room temperature. Freeze until solid before filling the molds with the cashew filling, approximately 1 hour.

TO MAKE THE FILLING:

Combine all ingredients in a blender and puree until very smooth.

Pour filling into molds outfitted with Fruit Pie bases.

Let set in freezer until solid, approximately 1 hour.

Once solid, remove entirely when ready for frosting.

CONTINUED ON NEXT PAGE

FOR PURPLE:

Ube extract, as needed

FOR YELLOW:

Lemon extract, as needed

Yellow food coloring, as needed

TO MAKE THE TOPPING:

Combine egg whites with sugar and cream of tartar in a heatproof bowl, and set it over a pot half-filled with simmering water over low heat. *The base of the bowl should not be touching the water.*

Whisk egg whites over simmering water until the sugar has completely dissolved, and looks frothy, approximately 8 to 10 minutes. If you (carefully) touch the egg whites, you should not feel any sugar granules in between your fingers. Note: To ensure egg whites are pasteurized, heat your egg whites to 160°F.

Transfer mixture to a stand mixer outfitted with a whisk. Whisk egg mixture on medium-high speed until stiff peaks form, approximately 3 to 5 minutes.

Divide mixture into 2.

Add as much ube extract as needed for desired taste and color for purple pies.

Add as much lemon extract and yellow food coloring as needed for desired taste and color for yellow pies.

Transfer topping to piping bags outfitted with round tips.

TO ASSEMBLE:

Unmold frozen fruit pies to final serving plate(s).

Carefully pipe yellow or purple toppings to fruit pies in a tidy swirl.

Enjoy frozen, or let thaw at room temperature for approximately 15 minutes until soft, but still cool.

GURU PATHIK'S ONION BANANA JUICE

Prep Time: 5 minutes

Cook Time: 45 minutes

Yield: Approximately 2 cups

This drink is chakra cleansing but awful tasting! Guru Pathik insists that if you drink Onion Banana Juice enough times you'll learn to love it. I guess I still haven't fully acquired a taste for it, but at least its effects work quickly—and in small doses!

—Aang

2 tablespoons neutral oil

½ medium sweet onion, peeled and sliced

1 cup plus 2 tablespoons water

3 tablespoons sugar

1 medium banana, peeled and sliced

1 piece candied ginger

1 cup soy milk

1 cup cubed ice

½ teaspoon kosher salt

Heat oil in a small pan over medium until slick and shiny. Add the onion and reduce heat to medium-low. Cook, stirring intermittently, until onion is well caramelized, approximately 30 minutes. Remove from heat, and reserve.

Combine 2 tablespoons water and the sugar in a small pan over medium heat. Once sugar begins to bubble, approximately 2 minutes, add banana. Reduce heat to medium-low, stir and cook until banana is lightly brown and well caramelized all over.

Combine onion, banana, ginger, soy milk, the remaining 1 cup water, ice, and salt in a blender. Blend until very smooth. Serve immediately.

AIR TEMPLE TSAMPA

Prep Time: 1 minute
Cook Time: 5 minutes
Yield: 6 to 7 tsampa balls

Tsampa was my regular mid-training snack during long lessons with Monk Gyatso . It may look plain, but the making of tsampa is a process not to be missed; the young Air Nomads and I loved watching the monks roast the barley for tsampa by airbending in big whiffs of hot sand until the temple kitchens would be filled with its nutty scent.

—Aang

1 cup whole barley, washed and dried

Balance Butter Tea

Add barley to a heavy-bottomed medium pot over medium heat. Toast, stirring intermittently, until the grains have turned a medium brown and give off a nutty aroma, approximately 10 minutes. Remove from heat, and let cool completely.

Grind toasted barley into flour using a high-powered blender or flour mill.

Combine toasted barley powder with hot butter tea, mixing in small increments, to form a more solid snack-sized bite of tsampa or a more porridge-like tsampa. Serve with more butter tea.

BALANCE BUTTER TEA

Prep Time: 3 minutes
Cook Time: 8-11 minutes
Yield: 2 cups

Because us Air Nomads lived in such high altitudes, we always kept a steady supply of butter (or milk) tea available to keep our bodies warm and balanced. For a simple cup in the afternoon, just some milk and salt will do; when greeting our friends from the other air temples, the monks served up the nicest butter as a special sign of welcome.

—Aang

2 cups water

2 to 3 tablespoons Pemagul tea leaves (or substitute with pu-erh or Lapsang souchong, depending on desired intensity)

½ teaspoon kosher salt

2 tablespoons unsalted butter

1 to 2 teaspoons sugar

¼ cup cake flour or barley flour (optional)

In a small pot over high heat, bring water to a boil. Add tea leaves, reduce heat to medium, and let steep 3 minutes. Stir in salt, then remove from heat and strain tea leaves.

Combine tea, butter, and sugar in a blender. Blend until very smooth and frothy.

If using, toast cake or barley flour in a heavy-bottomed pan until lightly brown in color and nutty in flavor, 5 to 8 minutes. Stir flour into tea to thicken, if desired.

WATER TRIBES

Now that the Hundred Year War has finally ended, Water Tribe people are able to safely spread out beyond the poles for the first time in my life. Watching so many changes take place within the Water Tribes has become a regular occurrence at tribal functions, and a whole generation of Southern Water Tribe kids have grown accustomed to ingredients that were once rare imported luxuries.

In past times, Water Tribe food came almost exclusively from our oceans, save some ground harvests during the warmer seasons. Nothing was wasted, and everything would be carefully divvied up and kept on ice to be used or eaten for months afterward. Out of the waters came the most incredible things—sea prunes, crabs, squid, and infinite variations of seaweed to occupy seaweed experts into their next lifetime. When we cooked, we channeled the beat of the water into our food—gently moistening a steamed fish, dynamically swirling water to poach puffin-seals, rapidly bubbling a broth of fish bones to extract its milky residue.

Nowadays, so many more ingredients are coming from the Earth Kingdom and the Fire Nation. These are good, perhaps necessary, developments, but sometimes I have expressed concern to the Council that the delicate cuisine of the Water Tribes might fade.

I like to view Water Tribe food these days as a convergence of preservation and exploration. Especially as I'm writing down the recipes from Gran Gran, exactness is my first goal, followed by changes that adapt to the times. My greatest hope is that the other nations will enjoy these Water Tribe dishes as much as I do.

—Katara

SOKKA'S SALMON JERKY

Prep Time:
10 minutes (active),
12 hours (inactive)

Cook Time:
8-12 hours (inactive)

Yield: Serves 6-12

When Dad left to fight in the war, he entrusted me with his foolproof method of making salmon jerky. Alongside freeze-dried cucumberquats, this is an important form of sustenance for warriors of the Southern Water Tribe. I knew it was my responsibility to learn the process well and pass on the knowledge to future generations in case he didn't return. Every time Katara and I see him, I make a big batch for us all to eat together as we sip seaweed broth and tell war stories.

—Sokka

Three 1-by-3-inch pieces kombu, pulverized into powder

1 tablespoon kosher salt

1 tablespoon white sugar

1 pound high-quality salmon, skin-on, pin-boned, sliced into ½-inch strips

In a small bowl, combine kombu powder with salt and sugar. Toss salmon with kombu mixture until evenly coated. Let cure in the refrigerator for 12 hours.

Rinse salmon under cold water to remove kombu mixture, then pat dry with paper towels.

Place salmon in a single layer in a dehydrator lined with parchment paper. Dehydrate at 140°F for 8 to 12 hours or until desired consistency. (If you do not have a dehydrator, turn your oven to the lowest heat setting. Place your salmon on a parchment-lined sheet tray, and check your salmon jerky every 30 minutes or so, starting at 4 hours.)

Remove salmon jerky from dehydrator, and let cool completely. Store salmon jerky in an airtight container in the refrigerator for 2 to 3 months.

FRIED FISH BALLS ON A STICK

Prep Time: 30 minutes

Cook Time: 10 minutes

Yield: Approximately 15 fish balls (about 3 cups fish paste)

Fried Fish Balls on a Stick have it all: crispy coating, tender fish, and a sharp stick to poke things with after you're done eating. What could be better?

These morsels are the perfect snack to share around a warm fire.

—Katara

1 pound skinless, boneless fish fillet, chopped (use a mild fish like dover sole, halibut, or flounder for best results) (500 grams)

1 cup cold water (100 grams)

2 teaspoons kosher salt

2 teaspoons white sugar

1 teaspoon ground kelp

2 large egg whites

2 tablespoons cornstarch

Neutral oil, as needed

5 to 8 bamboo skewers

Combine fish with ½ cup cold water into a food processor and pulse until very smooth, approximately 2 to 3 minutes.

Transfer fish mixture to a stand mixer outfitted with the paddle. Add salt, sugar, kelp, and cornstarch, and mix on low until well-combined, approximately 2 to 3 minutes. Note: Make sure to scrape down the sides and bottom of the bowl so nothing remains unmixed.

Add egg whites and continue to mix until well-combined, approximately 2 minutes.

As mixer is running, drizzle cold water into mixture and continue to mix at medium speed until all the ½ cup water has been absorbed.

Increase speed to high and mix for 10 to 15 minutes, or until fish paste is extremely fluffy and smooth.

Carefully scoop and shape fish paste into round fish balls 1½-inch in diameter and drop into a medium pot of cold water. Note: Wet your hands before shaping fish balls to avoid sticking.

Bring pot of water with fish balls to a light simmer over medium heat, and cook for 5 minutes.

Drain and set fish balls on paper towels to dry and cool completely.

Heat oil in a large pot over medium heat to 400°F.

Fry fish balls in batches, taking care to not overcrowd the pot, until golden brown.

Remove fish balls and drain on paper towels.

Let cool and drain for 2 minutes on paper towels, then spear onto wooden skewers to serve, if desired.

GRAN GRAN'S SMOKED ARCTIC HEN LEGS

**Prep Time:
2 minutes (active),
8-12 hours (inactive)**

**Cook Time: 2 hours
20 minutes**

Yield: Serves 4

Gran Gran taught me how to make the most from every animal we caught in the South Pole, knowing we always needed to conserve and think about the future. Because Arctic hens were more readily available than others, we were able to have the most fun with them in different preparations. When I could find enough branches or dried grasses, Gran Gran would let me smoke the hen legs as a special treat. I still cherish the memories of setting up a small smoking pit and the warmth of the smolder toasting my hands and face.

—Katara

2 tablespoons dried shrimp, pulverized into powder

2 tablespoons kosher salt

2 teaspoons sugar

4 duck legs

In a medium bowl, toss together the shrimp powder, salt, and sugar. Coat the duck legs in salt mixture, and let cure in the refrigerator 8 hours or overnight.

Rinse the duck legs under water, and pat dry with a paper towel.

Set up a stovetop smoker, or a regular smoker, with the wood chips of your choice according to the manufacturer's instructions.

Gently smoke (on stovetop) or cold smoke (in smoker) duck legs until skin turns a medium brown, 15 to 20 minutes.

Preheat oven to 400°F. Place duck legs on a parchment-lined sheet tray, and roast until the thickest part of the thigh registers 165°F.

Turn broiler on high. Place duck legs on top oven rack, and broil until skin is crispy and well-browned. Remove from heat and let cool 5 minutes before slicing.

FOGGY SWAMP CHICKEN

Prep Time:
15 minutes (active),
8-12 hours (inactive)

Cook Time: 30 minutes

Yield: Serves 4

The foggy swamp isn't for everybody, but for some, you just know you're home when you're here. When I'm sitting in the banyan grove, I can feel how everything in the swamp—the critters, the roots of bamboo and rice, even the miniscule fish in the water—are linked together, drawing their life energy from the same source. When I compose my meals of these ingredients, their flavors just naturally mix together, changing from individual parts into a single, delicious meal. I'm writing down this recipe for others to use, but I should tell you: this dish isn't something you can ever completely replicate. See, this water—our cradle of life—adds a certain essence you just can't find outside the swamp.

—HUU

FOR THE CHICKEN:

3 boneless, skinless chicken thighs, cut into 1-inch-wide pieces

3 scallions, minced

¼ cup rice paddy herb, minced (or substitute 1 teaspoon lemon zest plus ½ teaspoon ground cumin)

½-inch piece galangal, peeled and minced

1 teaspoon kosher salt

¼ teaspoon sugar

FOR THE RICE:

1 cup water

2 teaspoons kosher salt

2 teaspoons fish sauce

½ teaspoon white sugar

1 cup glutinous rice

FOR ASSEMBLY:

12 to 16 bamboo leaves, fresh or rehydrated

Water

TO PREPARE THE CHICKEN:

In a large bowl, combine chicken with scallions, rice paddy herb, galangal, salt, and sugar, and mix thoroughly. Marinate 8 hours or overnight in refrigerator. Reserve.

TO MAKE THE RICE:

In a medium bowl, whisk together water, salt, fish sauce, and sugar until salt and sugar have dissolved.

Add sticky rice, and let soak 8 hours or overnight in refrigerator.

Drain rice from solution, and reserve.

TO ASSEMBLE AND COOK:

Overlap two bamboo leaves on top of each other in the same direction, with the rough, stemmed side of each leaf facing inward.

At about one third the length of the leaves, place your thumbs on the inside of the leaves and fold inward while tucking in the bottom half of the leaves to create a pocket crease with your third and ring finger.

Add 1½ tablespoons rice plus two pieces of chicken into the crease.

Fold over the remaining length of the leaves, using twine to secure the overhang tightly. Repeat until all rice and chicken are gone.

Fill a large pot halfway with water, and bring to a boil over high heat.

Place wrapped chicken in pot, lower the heat to low. Cover and let cook 30 minutes, or until rice and chicken are both completely cooked through.

Carefully cut the twine, unwrap the bamboo leaves, and serve!

BLUEBERRY COOKIES

Prep Time: 5 minutes

Cook Time:
15 minutes (active)
50 minutes (inactive)

Yield: Approximately 10 cookies

A lot of people don't realize that blueberries grow wild in the arctic. There's nothing more amazing than summertime in the South Pole when the sun barely sets on the horizon and the blueberries are everywhere! The end of the war has brought far more deliveries of Earth Kingdom flour to the Water Nation, and now we make cookies with wild blueberry, too.

—Katara

Approximately ½ cup lard or refined coconut oil, room temperature (80 grams)

Approximately ½ cup white sugar (90 grams)

2 cups fresh blueberries (330 grams)

1¼ cup all-purpose flour (200 grams)

1 teaspoon baking powder

¼ teaspoon kosher salt

Combine lard with sugar in a stand mixer outfitted with a paddle attachment. Cream together until smooth, approximately. 2 to 3 minutes.

Place blueberries in a microwave-safe bowl and heat on high for 2 minutes, until jammy. Let cool 2 minutes, then pour into mixing bowl.

Mix together lard and blueberries until smooth.

Gradually add flour, baking powder, and salt. Mix until smooth.

Chill batter in refrigerator for 30 minutes or until more easily shapeable.

Preheat oven to 350F.

Shape cookie batter by hand into approximately 2½-inch flat discs.

Place cookies on parchment-lined sheet tray with at least 1-inch space in-between them.

Bake for 15 minutes, or until cookie is no longer doughy at center but soft and cake-like.

Remove from oven and let cool 2 minutes.

LIGHTLY PICKLED FISH

Prep Time:
12-16 hours (inactive)

Cook Time: 5 minutes

Yield: Serves 2

The Ember Island Players may have mocked me with pickled fish, but let me tell you, it is divine. And it's so easy, it's one of the first fish dishes Gran Gran entrusted me to make without Katara's supervision. I guess she felt even I couldn't mess it up *that* badly.

—Sokka

FOR THE PICKLING SOLUTION:

1 cup white vinegar

½ cup water

2 tablespoons whole juniper berries

3 teaspoons kosher salt

3 teaspoons white sugar

FOR THE FISH:

1-pound skinless, de-boned fish fillets of choice, cubed (use a hardy, meatier, oilier fish like kanpachi for best results)

TO MAKE THE PICKLING LIQUID:

Combine white vinegar, water, juniper, salt, and sugar in a small pot over medium heat.

Bring mixture to a boil, then reduce heat to medium-low and let cook 5 minutes.

Remove mixture from heat and transfer to a heat-safe container. Let steep until it cools to room temperature, then let infuse 8 hours or overnight in the refrigerator.

TO MAKE THE FISH:

Pour pickling solution over cubed fish until fish is covered.

Let pickle 4 hours or until fish has firmed up and turned a solid white, then strain to remove solution.

STEWED SEA PRUNE SOUP

Prep Time: 10 minutes

Cook Time: 1 hour, 30 minutes

Yield: Serves 4

Talk about a taste of home! I didn't think I would taste stewed sea prunes for quite some time after Sokka and I first left the Southern Water Tribe, so when Bato made them for us, I must've drunk at least five bowls in a single sitting. Gran Gran taught me that for ultra-creamy soup, you have to keep the broth boiling all afternoon, so Zuko's been helping me firebend a flame with great precision. If you're really hungry, you can add small chunks of sausage to make it a one-dish meal.

—Katara

FOR THE BROTH:

¼ cup neutral oil

2 pounds whole fish of choice, scaled, gutted, rinsed, dried, and chopped into 3 to 4 pieces

Kosher salt, as needed

½ yellow onion, peeled, sliced

6 cloves garlic, peeled, sliced

1 duck carcass, split in half, or 1 duck head plus 2 duck wings and 2 duck feet

4 quarts water

FOR THE ADDITIONS:

1½ cup dried whole morel mushrooms

One 6-inch-by-6-inch piece dried fish maw, rehydrated, chopped into ½-inch pieces

1 cup chopped dandelion greens (optional)

Heat oil in a large pot over high heat until slick and shiny.

Liberally salt fish with salt, then place in a large pot to fry until golden brown on all sides and meat is cooked through, approximately 3 to 5 minutes each side.

Remove fish from pot and shred all meat from bones. Reserve.

Return fish bones to pot and continue to fry another 2 to 3 minutes.

Add onion, garlic, and duck with some more salt. Continue to fry another 5 to 8 minutes, until duck bones have browned.

Add water and bring entire mixture to a light simmer over medium-low heat, skimming the surface of scum as it forms. Skim 2 to 3 times, or until surface is clear.

Over high heat, bring the entire mixture to a rolling boil. Cover, and reduce heat to low (ensuring mixture is still boiling) and let cook 1 hour. Check the broth level intermittently, adding more water as needed.

After 1 hour, remove lid and check broth level. It should have reduced by roughly half, to yield approximately 2 quarts of broth. Season broth to taste.

Strain broth and add morels and fish maw.

Bring to a light simmer over medium-low heat, cover and let cook until morels are rehydrated and fish maw is cooked through and translucent, approximately 15 minutes.

Garnish soup with dandelion greens, if desired.

FIVE-FLAVOR SOUP

Prep Time: 20 minutes (active), 2-3 hours (inactive)

Cook Time: 2 hours 20 minutes

Yield: 2 quarts stock, serves 4

So much has changed since the war ended, and as much as I've embraced many new Water Nation practices, it's been comforting to have some stay the same. This broth is that five-flavored soup of my childhood, even as the noodles have evolved from thinly cut strips of seaweed to long ropes of wheat (from the Earth Kingdom) and algae (from warmer waters). Enjoying this soup never fails to remind me of home.

—Katara

FOR THE SPIRULINA NOODLES:

1½ cups bread flour, plus more for dusting (200 grams)

1 teaspoon green spirulina powder

1 teaspoon lye water

½ teaspoon kosher salt

Slightly less than ½ cup water (90 grams)

TO MAKE THE SPIRULINA NOODLES:

In a stand mixer outfitted with dough hook set on medium-low speed, combine flour, spirulina powder, lye water, and salt until well mixed. Note: Lye water is dangerous if ingested undiluted; keep out of reach of children and pets.

With the mixer running at medium speed, slowly drizzle in water. The dough will look very dry and crumbly at first—resist the urge to add more water! Over time, the dough will come together. Once the dough has become cohesive, place it on a lightly floured surface and knead into one dough mound. Wrap with plastic, and let rest 2 to 3 hours.

Set up pasta sheeter at the widest setting. Divide the dough into two pieces, shape into discs, and use a rolling pin to roll each to roughly the same thickness as the pasta sheeter setting.

Feed through the pasta sheeter, going through twice each time, until you reach three levels below the thinnest pasta sheeter setting. If you do not have a pasta sheeter, roll dough out by hand using a rolling pin until it is as thin as desired.

Fold dough in thirds, then in half, and roll it out again to the widest pasta sheeter setting. Repeat the previous step.

Optional: If you have the patience, fold the dough in thirds, then in half, and roll it out one more time to develop the gluten and elasticity of the dough.

Once sheeted, feed dough through a pasta cutter or simply cut by hand to the width of your choice.

Toss the noodles in rice flour to ensure they do not stick to one another.

If serving noodles immediately, reserve in refrigerator. Otherwise, freeze in one layer on a parchment-lined sheet tray and wrapped in plastic for up to 3 months.

CONTINUED ON NEXT PAGE

FOR THE FIVE FLAVOR SOUP BASE:

4 duck wings, split, or 1 duck carcass

1 whole dried fish

Two 2½-by-4-inch dried kombu strips

2 tablespoons dried bonito flakes

2 tablespoons dried baby shrimp

¼ cup dried anchovies

12 cups water

Kosher salt

Maple syrup

FOR TOPPING (OPTIONAL):

Sliced octopus

Poached fish fillets

Sautéed shrimp

Seaweed knots

TO MAKE THE FIVE-FLAVOR SOUP:

Preheat oven to 400°F. On a lined baking sheet, roast duck wings until well browned all over, approximately 15 minutes on each side.

In a large pot, combine duck with the dried fish, kombu, bonito flakes, baby shrimp, anchovies, and water. Bring to a light simmer over medium heat.

Once soup has been simmering for 5 minutes, remove kombu. (You can use this kombu to make seaweed noodles, dice it and add to other dishes, or even make tea from it!) Cover and let simmer 2 hours, intermittently skimming the broth.

After 2 hours, taste for saltiness. You can either reduce the soup base until you reach the desired level of saltiness, or simply add salt to taste. Add maple syrup to taste.

TO SERVE:

Ladle hot soup in serving bowls.

Blanch the noodles in boiling water. Strain and transfer to soup bowls.

Garnish soup with toppings of your choice.

KALE COOKIES

**Prep Time: 5 minutes (active),
8-12 hours (inactive)**

Cook Time: 15-18 minutes

Yield: 12 large cookies

During Team Avatar's travels during the war, I came up with a clever way to replicate the look of traditional Water Tribe seaweed cookies using ingredients from the Earth Kingdom. I wasn't sure they would even taste good together, but kale and chocolate proved to be a crowd-pleaser with the gang.

—Katara

FOR THE KALE:

1 tablespoon lard (or substitute neutral oil)

2 bunches (about 8 cups) dinosaur kale, stemmed and roughly chopped

½ teaspoon kosher salt

FOR THE COOKIES:

½ cup unsalted margarine, melted and cooled

⅔ cup light brown sugar

⅓ cup sugar

½ teaspoon kosher salt

1 large egg

1½ cups all-purpose flour

1 teaspoon baking powder

2 tablespoons cornstarch

¼ teaspoon fresh ground black pepper

¼ to ½ cup mini chocolate chips, as desired

TO PREPARE THE KALE:

Heat lard in a large skillet over medium. Add kale with salt, and sauté until kale has reduced in size considerably and leaves look cooked through and soft, 5 to 8 minutes.

Transfer kale to food processor, and pulse into fine pieces. Reserve.

TO MAKE THE COOKIES:

In a medium bowl, whisk together the margarine with sugars and salt until smooth. Add the egg, and whisk again until smooth.

In a separate small bowl, whisk together flour, baking powder, cornstarch, and black pepper.

Carefully fold flour mixture into margarine mixture until just combined, avoiding overworking the dough. Add kale and chocolate chips, and fold again until just combined.

Wrap the cookie dough bowl in plastic, and refrigerate for 8 hours or overnight to firm up.

Preheat oven to 350°F. Using a scoop or a large spoon, form 12 round hockey pucks of cookie dough 2 inches in diameter, and place them on a cookie sheet. Make sure to leave 2 inches of space on either side so cookies can expand in the oven.

Bake until cookies have set and turned light golden brown at the bottom. Let cool 2 minutes before serving.

YUE'S MOONCAKES

Prep Time: 35 minutes

Cook Time: 2 hours, 10 minutes

Yield: 12 cakes

After Princess Yue's great sacrifice to save the Moon Spirit and restore balance in the world, the Northern Water Tribes developed a special dessert to honor her life. These gracefully sweet cakes are meant to be consumed with the same love and tenderness that Yue showed to everyone while she was still with us. They are made from some of Yue's favorite roots and seeds, all growing abundantly in the Spirit Oasis waters, and encased in a beautiful jade skin like the gentle light she shines upon us.

—Sokka

FOR THE LOTUS SEED PASTE:

(or substitute store-bought)

Two 15-ounce cans lotus seeds in water, drained and rinsed

Cold water

½ cup water, plus more if needed

3 tablespoons sugar

¼ teaspoon kosher salt

3 tablespoons lard (or coconut oil)

FOR THE SWEET TARO PASTE:

(or substitute store-bought)

1 large taro, peeled, chopped, steamed until very soft

2 tablespoons sugar

One 13½-ounce can full fat coconut milk

FOR THE SWEETENED WATER CHESTNUTS:

¼ cup sugar

20 water chestnuts from the can, drained

TO MAKE THE LOTUS SEED PASTE:

Place lotus seeds in medium pot with enough water to cover by 2 inches, and bring to a boil. Boil for 30 minutes. Strain and transfer to a food processor.

Add ½ cup water, sugar, and salt to the food processor. Process into a very smooth paste, adding more water 1 tablespoon at a time if necessary.

Heat 1 tablespoon of lard in a small heavy-bottomed pot (such as a cast iron) over medium heat until slick and shiny. Add lotus puree to cover the bottom of the pot, and fry gently over low heat, stirring intermittently, 10 minutes.

Add another 1 tablespoon of lard and continue to stir and fry, 10 minutes.

Add another 1 tablespoon of lard and continue to stir and fry, 10 minutes or until lotus paste has given up all its water, thickened considerably, and is now stiff enough to shape.

Remove from heat, let cool, and reserve in refrigerator.

TO MAKE THE SWEET TARO PASTE:

Combine taro, sugar, and milk in a medium heavy-bottomed pan over medium-low heat. Cook, stirring intermittently, mashing together the taro to let it slowly fry and thicken, 20 to 30 minutes.

Continue cooking, stirring, and mashing until the taro is stiff enough to shape.

Remove from heat, let cool, and reserve in refrigerator.

TO PREPARE THE SWEETENED WATER CHESTNUTS:

Melt sugar (by itself) in a small pot over medium heat until it is lightly brown. Note this will take a while, and the sugar will first look cakey and crystallized before suddenly melting. Keep your eye on the sugar, and stir it intermittently.

Once the sugar has melted, remove from heat and immediately add water chestnuts. Stir to combine.

Transfer mixture to a small container, and let cool completely. Reserve.

CONTINUED ON NEXT PAGE

FOR THE DOUGH:

Slightly more than ½ cup glutinous rice flour (75 grams)

Slightly more than ⅛ cup rice flour (25 grams)

¼ cup cornstarch (35 grams)

½ cup powdered sugar (60 grams)

¼ teaspoon kosher salt

½ cup whole milk

1 cup neutral oil (20 grams)

¼ teaspoon Osmanthus syrup (2 grams) (optional)

¼ drop blue food coloring (optional)

TO MAKE THE DOUGH:

Stir together glutinous rice flour, rice flour, cornstarch, powdered sugar, and salt in a medium bowl to remove any clumps.

Add milk, oil, and Osmanthus syrup (if using), and stir into a loose batter.

If using, add enough food coloring to make the batter a very light green-blue, jade-like color. (This is best achieved with blue food coloring rather than green.)

Transfer batter to an oven-safe bowl, and place in a steamer. Cover and let steam 20 minutes, or until a knife inserted into the batter can be removed cleanly.

Immediately transfer dough to a cutting board, and knead until very smooth using gloved hands. (It will be very hot at this point, so be careful!) Wrap dough in plastic, and let cool in refrigerator for 30 minutes or until cool to the touch.

Roll dough into a long log, and section into evenly sized pieces (the number will vary depending on the size of your mooncake molds). Flatten dough pieces with a rolling pin, and use a ring cutter to cut out circles of dough to encase the filling.

TO ASSEMBLE:

Scoop some taro or lotus filling and roll into a ball. (The amount will depend on the size of your mooncake mold.) Make an indent in the filling ball with your thumb, and place the candied water chestnut inside. Cover it with filling, and roll back into a ball.

Place the filling ball at the center of flat dough piece, and gently tug and pinch to seal the dough around the filling.

Place the dough ball with filling on a clean surface, and gently push to flatten it with a mooncake mold press. If your dough ball seems a little too wide, you can use both hands to rub the dough ball to increase the height while decreasing the width. Lift the mold press and gently push out the mooncake. Mooncakes are best served within a day.

SPIRIT OASIS TEA

Prep Time:
10 minutes (active),
8-12 hours (inactive)

Cook Time: 5-10 minutes

Yield: Serves 2

Water from the Spirit Oasis has magical healing properties meant for only the severest of injuries, not to be used lightly. Thus, those paying respects to the Spirit Oasis drink a different cleansing beverage—made from ingredients growing in its lush landscape—when meditating inside. I find drinking a cup calms my mind, letting me focus more thoughtfully on my breath, each exhale bringing me a little closer to my spiritual center.

—Katara

FOR THE TISANE:

1 large stalk lemongrass, stemmed, outer peel removed, whites only, chopped

3 slices galangal, peeled

2 teaspoons sugar

1½ cups boiling water

1 teaspoon rose water

Butterfly pea extract, as needed

FOR THE ICE CUBES:

Juice of half a satsuma or orange

Cold water

TO MAKE THE TISANE:

Combine lemongrass, galangal, and sugar in a heatproof glass or bowl. Add boiling water and stir.

Let cool and stir in rose water. Add enough butterfly pea extract to turn the entire concoction a light blue. Let infuse for 8 hours or overnight in the refrigerator.

TO MAKE THE ICE CUBES:

Divide satsuma juice among four standard-sized ice-cube molds. Fill molds with cold water. Freeze overnight or until solid.

TO SERVE:

Offer guests a cup with satsuma ice. Slowly pour the tisane, and watch it turn from blue to pink!

EARTH KINGDOM

The Earth Kingdom is *huge*, so you can't expect me to tell you about every single place when I haven't seen any of it. Remember the part where I'm blind? But I have tasted lots of different dishes so I can tell you all about that. If you want to learn about Earth Kingdom food, you'll just have to travel across it and experience it yourself.

Just so you know, all the different parts of the Earth Kingdom have special foods that are hard to re-create elsewhere—another reason you'll have to go there to try it all. Come to my parents' mansion in Gaoling or any of their friends' estates in the Upper Ring of Ba Sing Se, and you'll be served a totally unnecessary procession of meats and side dishes, *and* that expensive white rice they like—tons of fancy stuff outfitted in gravies and sauces simultaneously salty and sweet that our private chefs will have been cooking for days.

Start moving west, and everything turns significantly more sour and sometimes spicy. The foods smell really strong and delicious there. Trust me. I have a heightened sense of smell and I know what smells amazing. Then once you get to the desert, it's a totally different mix of scents—and flavors—altogether. The spices there are some of my favorites, just a sprinkle packs a punch—just like me. And in the forested areas, you find tons of wild game that's equally good spit-roasted or smoldered underground in clay or dirt (the most earthbendiest of the cooking styles, in my opinion).

If you visit the islands of the Earth Kingdom, you'll probably notice a lot more seafood (duh!) and also influences of the Fire Nation, since they're closer. Plus, many parts of the Earth Nation were annexed by the Fire Nation during the war, so with the villagers living and cooking together, it's unsurprising that dishes were blended together. I guess Aang is right—food really does bring people together. If you want a real culinary history of the Earth nation, go talk to that cabbage merchant. He's been touring this country from the back of his rickshaw since the first time we saw him in Omashu.

—TOPH

AUNT WU'S BEAN CURD PUFFS

Prep Time: 10 minutes

Cook Time: 5 minutes

Yield: Approximately 24 puffs

So maybe don't eat 15 of these in one sitting, since they tend to expand in your belly, but Aunt Wu's Bean Curd Puffs are the absolute best in the Earth Kingdom! I've been bugging the whole crew to make a pit stop in Makapu Village ever since the war ended, but they just won't listen to me. Looking back, it's a good thing Aang wasn't too interested in partaking, because I know Meng would've hoarded them for him and left me with none.

—Sokka

FOR THE SAVORY TARO PASTE:

2 tablespoons flavorful fat of any kind (lard, bacon fat, tallow)

6 cloves garlic, sliced

1-inch knob fresh ginger, peeled and sliced

5 scallions, whites only, sliced

1 tablespoon fermented black beans, minced

Kosher salt

4 cups (450 grams) taro, peeled, chopped, and steamed until very soft

1 teaspoon sugar

1 teaspoon white vinegar

FOR ASSEMBLY:

Fried tofu puffs

Savory tart paste, from above, as needed

Neutral oil, as needed

TO MAKE THE SAVORY TARO PASTE:

Heat fat in a small sauté pan over medium until slick and shiny. Add garlic, ginger, scallions, black beans, and a pinch of salt, and sauté until fragrant, 2 to 3 minutes.

Remove from heat, and transfer to a food processor. Process until minced, scraping down the sides once or twice. Add the taro to the food processor with sugar and vinegar. Process to combine thoroughly. Season with salt to taste.

Remove from the food processor, and reserve.

TO ASSEMBLE:

Score fried tofu puffs with an "X" and carefully remove the innards with a spoon, leaving the outside flap intact.

Stuff tofu puffs with savory taro paste, and re-seal with the outside flap.

Heat oil to 375°F.

Fry tofu puffs in oil until well-crisped on the outside, and taro is warmed on the inside. *Take care not to overcrowd the oil with too many tofu puffs at once.*

Drain on paper towels. Let cool 2 minutes before serving.

FREEDOM FIGHTERS ROAST PORK BELLY

Prep Time:
10 minutes (active),
8-12 hours (inactive)

Cook Time:
30-35 minutes

Yield: Serves 6-8

For all his faults, I still miss Jet a lot. He was the first person ever to take care of me, and just like Aang, he wanted to change the world for the better. I think his heart was always in the right place, even if it sometimes took a few detours. When we were able to catch small boars near our treetop hideouts outside of Gaipan, Jet taught me how to roast them over a spit until they were pleasantly crackly outside yet still soft inside. I miss those celebrations a lot, so I keep perfecting my boar-making skills as a small way of remembering him and our whole crew.

—THE DUKE

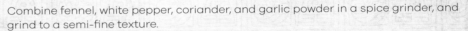

FOR THE SPICE RUB:

1 teaspoon whole fennel seed

1 teaspoon whole white pepper

1 teaspoon whole coriander seed

½ teaspoon garlic powder

FOR THE PORK BELLY:

2-pound pork belly slab

2 tablespoons soy sauce

2 tablespoons Shaoxing wine

1 teaspoon white sugar

Large rock salt, as needed

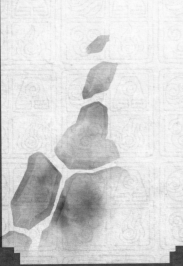

Combine fennel, white pepper, coriander, and garlic powder in a spice grinder, and grind to a semi-fine texture.

Using a sharp paring knife or ice pick, poke hundreds of small holes into the skin of the pork belly without exposing the flesh. This will help the pork belly crisp up.

Place pork belly flesh-side-down in flat food-safe container and rub with soy sauce and Shaoxing.

Rub spice rub and sugar onto pork belly flesh.

Flip pork belly to be skin-side-up, and blot dry with paper towels.

Let pork belly air-dry in refrigerator 8 hours or overnight.

Preheat oven to 350°F.

Place pork belly skin-side-up on an oven-safe tray lined with aluminum foil. Gently fold aluminum foil against the sides of the pork belly, encasing it like in a box with some foil peeking above all sides.

Pour a layer of large rock salt on the skin of the pork belly, covering it completely.

Roast pork belly until the insides registers 165°F, approximately 25 to 30 minutes.

Remove from oven and scrape off all rock salt, and flatten the sides of foil.

Preheat oven broiler to high.

Place pork belly, skin-side-up, under broiler. Let broil until skin crisps up dramatically.

Remove from oven and let cool 5 minutes before slicing.

GABLING TEA EGGS

Prep Time: 5 minutes

**Cook Time:
22–27 minutes**

Yield: 8 eggs

These richly flavored Tea Eggs were always great for picnics with badgermoles, sometimes they ate the eggs so fast I didn't get any, which is why I always kept a secret stash in my room at home. All that safekeeping really served me well, because tea eggs were in high demand during our long journeys on Appa's back—if I hadn't kept some for myself, Sokka would've eaten all of them! As long as you have plenty to go around, these are perfect for sharing with friends.

—TOPH

FOR THE MARINADE:

1 cinnamon stick

1 teaspoon Sichuan peppercorns

1 teaspoon white peppercorn

8 whole cloves

1 teaspoon fennel seed

5 whole star anise

1 teaspoon whole green cardamom

1 dried tangerine peel

1-inch knob fresh ginger, sliced

4 cloves garlic, sliced

1 scallion, chopped

4 cups water

3 tablespoons Lapsang souchong (or 5 tea bags)

1½ cups soy sauce

1 teaspoon white sugar

1 teaspoon toasted sesame oil

8 large eggs

Water, as needed

Combine the dried spices, tangerine peel, ginger, garlic, scallion, and water in a medium pot over medium heat. Bring to a light simmer, and let cook 15 minutes.

Bring mixture to a boil, then turn off heat. Add the Lapsang in a tea infuser, and let steep 10 minutes. Taste, and let steep longer if desired—the mixture should be lightly tannic (oversteeped) but not too bitter. Remove Lapsang. Add soy sauce, sugar, and sesame oil, and set mixture aside.

Fill a separate large pot with enough water to cover 8 eggs. Bring to a rolling boil. Gently add the eggs, and boil 7 to 12 minutes, depending on desired yolk consistency. For barely set centers, opt for 8 minutes.

Shock eggs in an ice-water bath, and let cool.

Gently crack eggs by tapping the tops and bottoms then rolling them along the counter.

Place eggs in marinade, and let marinate for 3 to 7 days in the refrigerator, depending on desired intensity. (Starting at 3 days, peel an egg and sample it!)

BEIFONG BEEF

Prep Time:
30 minutes (active),
2 hours (inactive)

Cook Time: 15 minutes

Yield: Serves 2-4

The uppity elites of the Earth Nation love to eat red meat. Beef, lamb, you name it. Usually, they make a big fuss about presenting the dish at the very end of the food processional, so everyone can ooh and aah at some special cut the host acquired that day. The fanciest is this beef stir-fry, which originated from the capital city. Okay, I'll admit, it *is* pretty tasty, and fine, yes, it's very tender and juicy. I had my family chef write down the recipe for this dish so Katara could make it for me and our friends.

—Toph

FOR THE BEEF:

1 pound beef flank, sliced against the grain into ¼-inch strips

1 teaspoon baking soda

FOR THE MARINADE:

1 tablespoon oyster sauce

1 tablespoon soy sauce

2 teaspoons cornstarch

2 teaspoons toasted sesame oil

1 tablespoon Shaoxing wine

FOR THE STIR-FRY:

3 tablespoons neutral oil (or substitute roasted rapeseed oil, if you are really fancy)

4 cloves garlic, minced

Two 1-inch knobs fresh ginger, peeled and minced

1 tablespoon fermented black beans, minced

1 large sweet onion, peeled and sliced

2 green bell peppers, sliced

2 red bell peppers, sliced

Soy sauce

¼ cup Shaoxing wine

Sugar (optional)

½ teaspoon fresh ground black pepper

1 teaspoon toasted sesame seeds

TO TENDERIZE THE BEEF:

Rub beef with baking soda until thoroughly coated. Place in a nonreactive container, cover with plastic wrap, and refrigerate for 1 hour or up to 2 hours.

TO MARINATE THE BEEF:

Remove beef from container, and wash thoroughly under cold water. Pat dry with clean paper towels, and transfer to a new container. Marinate beef at least 1 hour, or up to 24 hours.

TO MAKE THE STIR-FRY:

Heat the wok on high until smoking. If using a sauté pan, add oil to pan instead of heating just the pan. Add oil, swirling to coat the wok.

Working quickly, add garlic, ginger, and black beans, and stir for 5 seconds. They will cook and brown very rapidly. Immediately add marinated beef, and stir to coat. Keep cooking beef until all sides are well browned, approximately 3 minutes. Add onion and bell peppers with a splash of soy sauce. Let cook 1 minute.

Deglaze the wok or pan with Shaoxing wine. Let cook until most of the wine has evaporated, approximately 2 minutes. Start tasting your beef, and add more soy sauce or sugar if needed. Once finished, remove beef from heat, and add black pepper. Stir to thoroughly coat.

Plate the stir-fry, and garnish with sesame seeds.

UNCLE IROH'S JOOK

Prep Time:
2 minutes (active),
10-15 hours (inactive)

Cook Time:
30-45 minutes

Yield: Serves 5

My uncle makes the absolute best jook, even though he's not from the Earth Kingdom. I think it has something to do with those little yellow grains he puts in when no one's looking (I won't tell anyone, Uncle!), or maybe it's his ability to keep the fire at just the right heat when cooking. A bowl of Uncle's jook always brightens me up when I'm sick or feeling down; just the sight of all those fixings puts me in a better mood.

—Zuko

FOR THE JOOK:

1 cup brown rice

½ cup millet

12 cups water

1 teaspoon kosher salt

Chopped fresh cilantro, for garnish

Chopped toasted peanuts, for garnish

FOR THE SCALLION OIL:

1 bunch scallions, roughly chopped

¾ cup neutral oil

FOR THE DOUGH STICKS:

2½ cups all-purpose flour (300 grams)

½ teaspoon baking soda

1½ teaspoons baking powder

½ teaspoon kosher salt

1 teaspoon sugar

1 large egg

1 tablespoon neutral oil (15 grams)

½ cup cold water (130 grams)

Neutral oil, for frying

TO MAKE THE JOOK:

Combine rice, millet, and water in a large pot over medium-low heat.

Bring to a light simmer, then cover and cook over low heat until rice and millet have taken on desired consistency, about 30 to 35 minutes.

Add salt, stir, and serve with desired accompaniments.

TO MAKE THE SCALLION OIL:

Combine scallions with oil in a small pot over medium heat.

Cook until scallions begin to sizzle lightly, approximately 5 minutes.

Reduce heat to low, and cook another 5 to 10 minutes or until scallion greens have dulled.

Remove from heat, and let infuse another 15 minutes.

Strain scallions from oil, and reserve the oil.

TO MAKE THE DOUGH STICKS:

Combine all ingredients in a stand mixer fitted with the dough hook set on medium-low speed. Mix and knead until dough is supple and elastic, approximately 8 minutes. Remove the dough, and wrap in plastic. Let rest 8 hours or overnight in the refrigerator.

Remove dough from refrigerator, and bring to room temperature, 2 to 3 hours. Divide dough in half. Roll each dough half into a rectangle about ¼-inch thick, then slice into 8 pieces widthwise.

Stack two slices of dough of roughly the same size together, then use a chopstick to press a long divot into the dough stack lengthwise. Repeat for all slices of dough.

Grasp each end of finished dough slices with your hands, and pull them gently to stretch to double the original length. Set aside.

In a large, heavy-bottomed pot, heat frying oil to 400°F. Add dough slices a few at a time, not overcrowding the pot, and fry until golden brown. Make sure to turn the dough slices so all sides are fried. Drain on paper towels.

Dough sticks should be served immediately or cooled completely, then frozen. Dough sticks will keep in the freezer for up to 3 months. Reheat at 350°F until warmed through.

SONG'S ROAST DUCK

Prep Time:
30 minutes (active),
4-24 hours (inactive)

Cook Time: 65-75 minutes

Yield: Serves 4

I've never had roast duck like the one prepared by Song's mother. What a rapturous meal that was! I keep requesting the chefs of the Fire Nation palace replicate it as a special dish to accompany National Tea Appreciation Day, but they keep stalling on me. Something about the ducks being different here. I guess I'll just have to reserve my roast-duck-eating for when I'm back at the shop in Ba Sing Se.

—Iroh

FOR THE SPICE RUB:

8 whole star anise

1 cinnamon stick

2 pieces whole sand ginger (optional)

10 whole green cardamom

6 whole white cardamom

3 whole black cardamom

1 teaspoon whole black pepper

FOR THE MARINADE:

2 tablespoons neutral oil

2 stalks scallions, stemmed and sliced

1-inch knob fresh ginger, peeled and sliced

1 tablespoon Shaoxing wine

1 tablespoon soybean sauce

1 tablespoon shoisin

2 teaspoons light brown sugar

1 tablespoon soy sauce

1 tablespoon spice rub from above

FOR THE DUCK:

1 Peking duck, head and feet removed, patted dry

Kosher salt, as needed

FOR THE GLAZE AND ASSEMBLY:

¼ cup maple syrup

2 tablespoons white vinegar

1 tablespoon soy sauce

1 tablespoon spice rub, from above

TO MAKE THE SPICE RUB

Grind all spices in a spice grinder until medium-coarse.

TO MAKE THE MARINADE:

Heat oil in small skillet over medium heat until slick and shiny.

Add scallions and ginger, sauté 2 to 3 minutes or until fragrant.

Add Shaoxing wine and let cook 30 seconds.

Add soybean sauce, hoisin, brown sugar, soy sauce, and spice rub, and cook 2 to 3 minutes, stirring until well combined.

Remove from heat and let cool.

TO MAKE THE DUCK:

Liberally rub duck all over with kosher salt. Let stand at room temperature 30 minutes.

Bring a large of water to a rolling boil. Blanch duck in water, ladling hot water over any parts of duck that may not be submerged, 2 to 3 minutes or until duck skin has visibly contracted and looks taut and firm.

Carefully remove duck from water and place on a resting rack with breast side up.

Carefully pour marinade into duck cavity.

Let duck cool to room temperature, then transfer to refrigerator. Let duck sit, uncovered, in refrigerator to dry out its skin, a minimum of 4 hours and up to 24 hours.

Remove duck from refrigerator and carefully truss, taking care not to spill the marinade.

TO ASSEMBLE:

Combine all ingredients in small skillet over medium heat.

Bring to a light simmer, and let mixture reduce for 2 to 3 minutes until it has thickened slightly, to the consistency of a demi-glace.

Brush liberally over trussed duck.

Preheat oven to 400°F.

Place duck in middle rack of oven, with a shallow pan of boiling water on a lower rack to create some steam.

Roast duck for 25 minutes, re-glazing once halfway through.

Reduce the oven temperature to 350°F. Continue to cook duck, re-glazing every 10 minutes, until an internal thermometer inserted at the thickest part of the thigh registers 165°F, approximately 30 to 40 minutes.

Remove duck from oven and let rest 10 minutes before carving.

SEARED FISH

Prep Time: 5 minutes

Prep Time: 5 minutes
Cook Time: 15 minutes
Yield: Serves 4

The Kyoshi Warriors tell me there was once a pirate traveling all over the world, who learned the secrets for cooking the giant fish roaming near Kyoshi Island. At some point in his journey, he made his way to the northwestern parts of the Earth Kingdom, where he learned techniques from the Hami tribe and other expert benders in the area. Now you can find this dish in restaurants all over the Earth Kingdom. Who knew these whiskered fish could taste so good?

—TOPH

FOR THE SAUCE:

2 tablespoons neutral oil

½ medium yellow onion, minced

5 cloves garlic, minced

5 stalks Chinese celery, minced

1 green bell pepper, diced

2 teaspoons ground cumin

1 teaspoon whole caraway seeds

3 roma tomatoes, diced

½ teaspoon fresh ground black pepper

Black vinegar

Kosher salt

Sugar

FOR THE SEARED FISH:

2 pounds catfish, cut into steaks

Kosher salt

Cornstarch, for dredging

Neutral oil, for frying

TO MAKE THE SAUCE:

Heat the oil in a medium rondeau or skillet over medium until slick and shiny. Add the onion and garlic. Sauté 1 to 2 minutes or until fragrant. Add celery and bell pepper. Sauté 3 to 5 minutes or until bell pepper is beginning to soften. Add cumin and caraway seed. Sauté another minute. Add tomatoes and black pepper, and cook 8 to 10 minutes or until moisture from the tomato has almost evaporated and the vegetable mixture is beginning to become tacky.

Remove from heat. Season with black vinegar, salt, and sugar to taste, and set aside.

TO MAKE THE FISH:

Preheat oven to 400°F. Liberally salt the fish, then dredge each piece in cornstarch, and dust off excess.

Heat a thin layer of oil in a large oven-safe, heavy-bottomed pan over medium until slick and shiny. Sear the catfish steaks on all sides until lightly golden brown.

Transfer catfish in pan into hot oven, and cook until an internal thermometer reads at least 135°F. Remove catfish from pan, and let rest 3 minutes before serving with sauce.

SOUR CABBAGE SOUP

What kind of soup would be worthy of my prized cabbages? I traveled far and wide across the Earth Nation for an answer to this question. Finally, in the southwest, I found my answer: an iron-green broth with mouth-puckering sourness from mustard greens, tingly ma la from green peppercorns, and creamy depth from the claws of ducks. It was the perfect lure for weary travelers to stop into the Cabbage Delicacies Restaurant for an early supper.

—cabbage merchant

FOR THE STOCK:

1 pound chicken or duck feet (or substitute 2 chicken carcasses)

½ medium yellow onion, sliced

4 cloves garlic, sliced

2 teaspoons green Sichuan peppercorns

1 tablespoon kosher salt

1 teaspoon sugar

1 tablespoon white vinegar

10 cups water

FOR THE SOUP:

2 tablespoons neutral oil

8 cloves garlic, minced

2 scallions, minced

1-inch knob fresh ginger, peeled and minced

1 tablespoon doubanjiang (fermented fava bean paste, optional)

⅔ cup store-bought pickled mustard greens, thinly sliced

5 store-bought pickled chiles, minced (optional)

8 shiitake mushroom caps, sliced

1 head napa cabbage or green cabbage, cored and chopped

Kosher salt

Sugar

Ground white pepper

Chopped fresh cilantro, for garnish

TO MAKE THE STOCK:

Combine all ingredients in a pressure cooker, and pressure-cook on high for 1 hour. Let pressure release naturally. Strain, cool, and reserve.

If pressure cooker is not available, combine all ingredients in large pot, and bring to a low simmer over medium, skimming as needed. Cover and continue simmering over low heat, 4 to 6 hours. Strain, cool, and reserve.

TO MAKE THE SOUP:

In large pot, heat oil over medium heat until slick and shiny. Add garlic, scallions, and ginger, and sauté 1 to 2 minutes until fragrant. Add doubanjiang, if using, and sauté another minute. Add pickled mustard greens and chiles, sauté another minute.

Add 6 to 8 cups reserved chicken stock, and increase heat to high. Bring to a light simmer. Add mushrooms and cabbage. Cook until cabbage has softened and is translucent, 8 to 10 minutes.

Season to taste with salt, sugar, and white pepper. Garnish with cilantro, if desired, and serve.

CHARRED CABBAGE NOODLES

Prep Time:
15 minutes (active),
1 hour (inactive)

Cook Time: 3½–4½ hours

Yield: Serves 2-3

People ask me all the time if I tire of eating my cabbages, and I'm incredulous at the thought. Do they ask rabaroos if they want to stop eating cabbage? I think not! Besides, how can I bore of cabbage when there are so many ways to cook it? Take this cabbage-and-noodle goodness I dreamed up while traveling through the northwestern lands of the Earth Kingdom—why would you want anything else for dinner when you can have this plate of cabbage?

—cabbage merchant

FOR THE LAMB:

Kosher salt

2 pounds boneless leg of lamb

2 tablespoons neutral oil

5 cloves garlic

½ medium yellow onion, quartered

3-inch knob fresh ginger, peeled and halved lengthwise

1 teaspoon white peppercorns

2 teaspoons red Sichuan peppercorns

1 teaspoon cumin seeds

7 star anise pods

1 cinnamon stick

1 teaspoon whole coriander seeds

1 cup sliced celery

½ cup chopped fresh cilantro stems (reserve leaves for garnish)

3 tablespoons Shaoxing wine

¼ cup soy sauce

1 tablespoon black vinegar

1 tablespoon maple syrup

2 cups water

TO MAKE THE LAMB:

Liberally salt the lamb. In a large, heavy bottomed pot or pressure cooker, heat oil on high until slick and shiny. Add lamb, skin-side-down, and sear until well-browned, about 2 minutes. Remove from heat. Remove the lamb from pot and set aside. Set aside pot to reserve lamb fat.

If you have a gas stove, set up a grilling grate over your largest burner. Place garlic, onion, and ginger on grate, and turn heat onto high. Char aromatics on all sides until blackened, then remove and reserve.

If you do not have a gas stove, place garlic, onion, and ginger on a sheet tray. Turn broiler to high, and place sheet tray on top level of oven. Broil until blackened, flipping once, 3 to 5 minutes.

Dry-toast all spices in a small skillet until fragrant, 3 to 4 minutes. Transfer spices to a spice sachet.

Reheat oil and lamb fat in the large pot over medium until slick and shiny. Add charred aromatics, celery, and cilantro. Sauté 2 to 3 minutes or until fragrant.

Deglaze with Shaoxing wine, and sauté another minute.

Add lamb, spice sachet, soy sauce, black vinegar, and maple syrup. Now, you can either:

- Add 2 cups of water, and pressure cook on high for 1 hour.
- Braise on the stovetop by adding enough water to cover the lamb, bringing the mixture to a simmer, then covering and letting cook 2 to 3 hours or until tender and easily shredded by a fork.

If cooking via pressure cooker, once time is up, release pressure naturally then continue to reduce cooking liquid using the "Sauté" function until reduced by half or yields about 2½ cups of liquid.

If cooking via braising, reduce the liquid until it yields roughly 2½ cups of liquid.

Strain lamb, reserving the liquid, and roughly shred with a fork.

Reserve lamb and liquid separately in the refrigerator.

CONTINUED ON NEXT PAGE

FOR THE NOODLES (OR SUBSTITUTE STORE-BOUGHT):

⅓ cup all-purpose flour

10 tablespoons wheat starch (100 grams)

¼ teaspoon kosher salt

1½ cups cold water (340 grams)

Neutral oil

FOR ASSEMBLY:

4 tablespoons neutral oil, divided

4 cloves garlic, minced

1-inch knob fresh ginger, peeled and minced

¼ head napa cabbage, cored and chopped

½ teaspoon kosher salt

¼ cup Shaoxing wine

Soy sauce

Black vinegar

Sugar

Sliced scallions, for garnish

Chopped fresh cilantro, for garnish

TO MAKE THE NOODLES:

Whisk together the flour, starch, salt, and water. Let rest 1 hour, then whisk again to form a milky mixture.

Brush a shallow nonstick 9-by-13-inch cake pan with a thin layer of oil. Add half a cup of starchy water to the pan to form a very thin layer.

Steam over medium heat, covered, for 2 minutes or until the mixture turns translucent and is bubbly.

Place pan into ice-cold water to cool, and brush the top of the mixture with a thin layer of oil. Carefully remove mixture from pan with hands, and reserve on a plate.

Repeat until all the starchy water has been used.

Carefully roll steamed noodle sheets into jelly rolls, and slice to desired thickness of noodle. Reserve.

TO ASSEMBLE:

Heat 2 tablespoons of oil in a medium skillet or wok over high heat. Add the garlic and ginger. Sauté until fragrant, approximately 30 seconds. Add cabbage with salt. Continue to sauté until cabbage is lightly charred, approximately 5 minutes. Add Shaoxing wine, and cook another 2 minutes until extra liquid has evaporated. Transfer cabbage to a large bowl, and reserve.

Heat the remaining 2 tablespoons of oil in the same skillet or wok over high heat. Add the reserved cooked noodles, and sauté 2 to 3 minutes until lightly charred.

Add the reserved shredded lamb, and continue to sauté 2 to 3 minutes before adding the reserved braising liquid. Once the braising liquid is bubbling, add soy sauce, black vinegar, and sugar to taste.

Add the reserved cabbage, and stir together to combine.

Serve with scallions and cilantro as garnish.

COOKIE OF THE WHITE LOTUS

Prep Time:
10-12 minutes (active),
2 hours (inactive)

Cook Time: 25-30 minutes

Yield: 12-15 cookies

Even when the Order of the White Lotus is strategizing something seriously, we still know how to cultivate an atmosphere of fun and enjoyment. After all, what is life without some fun and games? Since we do not encourage gambling, the prize for Pai Sho players isn't money but a special Cookie of the White Lotus. These cookies are both crispy and crumbly and never last long once I pull them out of the oven. Winners get first pick, but everyone gets a cookie in the end.

—Iroh

FOR THE LOTUS PASTE:

One 14-ounce can of lotus seeds in water, drained, rinsed (yields 7 ounces lotus seeds)

½ cup water

2 tablespoons white sugar

1 tablespoon coconut oil

FOR THE COOKIES:

1 cup margarine, room temperature (225 grams)

½ cup white sugar (112 grams)

1 large egg yolk

¼ teaspoon kosher salt

1½ cups (225 grams) all-purpose flour

Powdered sugar (optional)

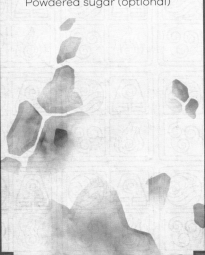

TO MAKE THE LOTUS PASTE:

Puree lotus seeds with water and sugar in a blender on high speed until very smooth.

Heat coconut oil in a medium skillet over low heat until slick and shiny.

Add lotus puree and "fry" puree ,removing its water content by continually flipping paste over on itself until it has dried considerably and can hold shape, approximately 8 to 10 minutes.

Remove and let cool to room temperature, then reserve in refrigerator. *Should yield about ¾ cup (255 grams) lotus paste.*

TO MAKE THE COOKIES:

Cream margarine and sugar in stand mixer outfitted with paddle until light and fluffy, approximately 2 to 3 minutes.

Add egg yolk and salt, and continue to mix 1 minute until combined.

Add flour, in 3 to 4 batches, mixing each time until fully combined.

Transfer dough to refrigerator and let cool 1 hour.

Halve dough, then place each half of dough between 2 sheets of parchment paper. Roll dough to about ¼-inch-thick rectangle.

Remove top sheet of parchment, and spread lotus paste along half of the dough rectangle.

Fold cookie dough without lotus paste onto the half with lotus paste, and gently flatten to seal.

Transfer cookie dough to freezer and freeze until solid, approximately 1 hour.

Preheat oven to 350°F.

Remove cookie dough from freezer and use cookie cutter to punch out to desired shapes. *Extra cookie dough can be re-molded and used, but it will not bake as evenly as the layers of cookie and lotus paste. It is best to bake the extra cookie dough as off in small cookie balls.*

Bake cookies on parchment-lined sheet pans until just barely golden brown, approximately 15 to 20 minutes.

Remove cookies from oven and let cool completely.

Dust with powdered sugar, if desired.

EARTHBENDER MUDSLIDE

The Boulder may still feel indignant at his loss in the Earth Rumble—again—to the Blind Bandit, but the Boulder also knows that warriors require rest. The Boulder is committed to recuperating with the Pebble and the Pebblets at home, and this drink will certainly do the trick.

—THE BOULDER

1 small banana

1 tablespoon toasted black sesame seeds

4 teaspoons cacao powder (not cocoa powder)

2 tablespoons unsalted creamy peanut butter

2 cups unsweetened soy milk

3 tablespoons maple syrup, plus more if needed

Combine all ingredients in blender, and blend until smooth. Add more maple syrup if you prefer a sweeter drink. Chill and serve cold.

MISTY PALMS SPECIAL RICE

Prep Time:
5 minutes (active),
30 minutes (inactive)

Cook Time:
Approximately 1 hour

Yield: Serves 3-5

While the Misty Palms Oasis didn't offer quite the vacation I was hoping for, at least it made up for it in good food and drink! While Toph and Sokka slurped down the mango and lychee nut ice smoothies, I had a few good helpings of the cantina's special rice before we went into the desert with Professor Zei. I'm so happy to see the town's been growing so actively these last few years despite its long mistreatment at the hands of the king and the Dai Li. I think by the next generation, the city will be restored, and citizens all over the kingdom will be clamoring to visit.

—Katara

FOR THE LAMB:

3 tablespoons neutral oil

1½ pounds boneless leg of lamb or lamb shoulder

Kosher salt, as needed

2 teaspoons whole coriander seed

2 teaspoons whole cumin seed

1 teaspoon whole black peppercorn

½ medium onion, peeled and sliced

4 cloves garlic, peeled and sliced

1-inch knob fresh ginger, peeled and sliced

2 large carrots, peeled and chopped

2 teaspoons kosher salt

1 teaspoon black vinegar

1 quart unsalted chicken or lamb stock

FOR THE RICE:

2 cups medium grain white rice

Cold water, as needed

2 tablespoons neutral oil

½ medium yellow onion, peeled and minced

5 cloves garlic, peeled and minced

2 carrots, peeled and diced small

½ teaspoon whole cumin seed

½ teaspoon whole fennel seed

¼ cup raisins

½ teaspoon kosher salt

Chopped lamb, from above

Stock, from above

¼ cup chopped dill

TO MAKE THE LAMB:

Heat oil in pressure cooker over high heat until slick and shiny.

Liberally rub lamb with salt, then brown in pot on all sides. Remove from pot and reserve.

Add coriander seed, cumin seed and black peppercorn to pot, and sauté 1 to 2 minutes, or until fragrant.

Add onion, garlic, ginger, carrots, and salt to pot. Sauté 3 to 5 minutes or until onion is translucent.

Add back lamb, vinegar, and stock.

Pressure cook for 20 minutes at high pressure, then let natural pressure release 10 minutes. *Alternatively, you can braise the lamb on a stovetop in a covered pot until tender, just make sure to add additional stock intermittently as it cooks.*

Remove lamb from pressure cooker and let cool. Chop into bite-sized ½-inch cubes.

Strain stock and reserve. You should have 1 quart of stock.

TO MAKE THE RICE:

Soak rice in cold water for 30 minutes. Strain and reserve.

Heat oil in a heavy-bottomed, medium pot or Dutch oven over medium heat until slick and shiny.

Add onion, garlic, and carrots, and sauté 2 to 3 minutes until fragrant.

Add cumin and fennel, sauté another 1 to 2 minutes.

Add raisins, rice, and salt. Stir together to combine.

Flatten the top of rice, and add chopped lamb to cover.

Add enough stock to just barely cover the rice. *Stock should not be covering the lamb.*

Cover pot and let cook on medium heat until rice has been cooked through and a nice crusty bottom has formed, approximately 25 to 30 minutes.

Garnish with dill, if desired.

LOTUS ROOT SALAD

Prep Time: 5 minutes
Cook Time: 10 minutes
Yield: Serves 1-2

I swear, Aang has a real knack for finding new foods to harry me with. At least this one I find tolerable—okay, fine, I rather like it. It's crunchy and juicy, with a funny little tingle I wasn't expecting. At any rate, it's whole lot better than those terrible raw kale wraps I always see him scarfing down like a lop-eared rabbit.

—TOPH

1 tablespoon kosher salt

2 fresh lotus roots, peeled and sliced thinly

¼ cup neutral oil

2-inch knob fresh ginger, peeled and minced

5 cloves garlic, minced

4 scallions, separated into greens and whites, minced

1 cup young pea sprouts

½ cup chopped fresh cilantro

2 tablespoons rice vinegar

2 teaspoons green Sichuan peppercorn oil

Kosher salt

Sugar

Bring a medium pot of water to a rolling boil, and add a pinch of salt. Blanch lotus root 1 to 2 minutes or until fully cooked through. Shock with ice water, drain, and reserve.

Heat the oil in a small pot to 325°F. In a small heatproof bowl, combine ginger, garlic, and scallion whites. Carefully pour the hot oil on top (it will sizzle), and mix to combine.

In a large bowl, toss together the lotus root, pea sprouts, cilantro, and scallion greens until thoroughly combined. Add in the ginger-garlic oil, rice vinegar, and Sichuan peppercorn oil, and toss to mix thoroughly. Season with salt and sugar to taste.

KYOSHI ISLAND STUFFED APPLE DONUTS

Prep Time:
15 minutes (active),
2½ hours (inactive)

Cook Time: 18-20 minutes

Yield: Approximately
10 donuts

All desserts have a place at the table for Kyoshi Day! After the warriors finish early training on our special holiday, we all take the afternoon and evening off to ready ourselves for the festivals that last from dusk till twilight. I think the stars of the show are the apple donuts, so I reserve mine for the final few minutes of the sunset, just as the last of the sun's rays are glimmering off the pillars of the Kyoshi Shrine.

—Suki

FOR THE DOUGH:

Approximately 1¼ cups all-purpose flour (155 grams)

Approximately 1¼ cups tapioca flour (155 grams)

2 tablespoons white sugar

¼ teaspoon kosher salt

1 tablespoon instant yeast

Approximately ⅓ cup warm milk, 105 to 110°F (80 grams)

2 tablespoons margarine, melted

1 large egg yolk

FOR THE FILLING:

2 gala apples, peeled, cored, and chopped (yields ~330 grams)

2 tablespoons white sugar

1 tablespoon water

1 teaspoon powdered matcha (preferably apple matcha)

FOR THE ICING:

2 tablespoon unsalted butter or margarine (30 grams)

¼ cup honey (85 grams)

1 cup powdered sugar (110 grams)

2 teaspoons matcha powder (preferably apple matcha)

TO MAKE THE DOUGH:

Whisk together all-purpose flour, tapioca flour, sugar, salt, and yeast in a suitably sized bowl.

Whisk together milk, margarine, and egg yolk in a separate bowl until well combined. Transfer to flour mixture.

Knead mixture 3 to 5 minutes until a dough forms, adding some extra all-purpose flour if necessary to prevent dough from sticking. It should be soft, but not sticky.

Cover bowl with plastic wrap, and let rise in a warm area (ideally 85°F) for 2 hours.

Transfer dough to a clean surface lightly dusted with flour.

Gently roll dough to approximately ½-inch thick. Use a cookie cutter of your choice to cut out dough, transferring finished circles to a parchment-lined sheet tray.

Repeat above step until all dough has been used. *You can reuse scraps by kneading them together and re-rolling them.*

Cover punched-out doughnuts with plastic, and let re-rise 30 minutes in a warm area (ideally 85°F).

Preheat oven to 375°F.

Bake doughnuts for approximately 10 minutes or until very puffy and golden brown.

Remove from oven, and let cool before filling and icing.

TO MAKE THE FILLING:

Combine apples, sugar, and water in a medium pot over medium-low heat.

Cook apple mixture until apples break down into smaller, chunky, cooked pieces, approximately 5 to 7 minutes .

Transfer apple mixture to blender and puree with matcha powder.

Transfer to food-safe container and let cool to room temperature. Reserve.

TO MAKE THE ICING:

Melt butter and honey in small pot over low heat, whisking to combine.

Once melted, add powdered sugar and matcha powder, whisking to combine.

Let cool 2 minutes before using. *If icing cools too quickly, gently re-warm over low heat.*

TO ASSEMBLE:

Pierce the side of the doughnut with a paring knife until roughly halfway through the donut.

Transfer apple filling to a piping bag, and pipe in filling into doughnut.

Dip the top side of doughnuts in icing, then let cool to harden.

JENNAMITE
AKA CREEPING CRYSTALS

Prep Time: 5 minutes

Cook Time: 20 minutes (active), approximately 1 week (inactive)

Yield: 6-8 rock candies

You know, jennamite is actually a really delicious candy when it's not trying to suffocate you. I personally like the green the best—it's not fair that's the one Katara got to eat!—but King Bumi says he is most fond of the yellow, because it also glows the brightest at night. The real question is: Why does such a useful rock have to be so dangerous?

—Sokka

FOR THE STICKS:

Water

Sugar

FOR THE SUGAR BASE:

1 cup water, plus more as needed

3 cups sugar, plus more as needed

FOR THE GREEN:

½ teaspoon pandan extract (optional)

1 drop green gel food coloring

FOR THE PURPLE:

½ teaspoon ube extract (optional)

1 drop purple gel food coloring

FOR THE YELLOW:

½ teaspoon lemon extract (optional)

1 drop yellow gel food coloring

SPECIAL SUPPLIES:

8 ice-pop sticks or skewers

8 tall glass jars

Clothespins

TO PREPARE THE STICKS:

Roll the ice-pop sticks or skewers in water, then in sugar, dusting off excess. Set aside to dry.

TO MAKE THE SUGAR BASE:

In a large pot over medium heat, bring water to a boil. Add sugar, 1 cup at a time, stirring until it is completely incorporated. The mixture will get very thick and syrupy and will turn slightly opaque.

Divide mixture among three heat-safe containers. Tint each a different color using extracts and food coloring. Let cool 10 minutes.

Rinse the jars in hot water very quickly.

Divide colors among the jars, making sure the jars are three-quarters filled.

Set up each jar with one stick held with a clothespin so it is directly at the center of the jar, immersed into the sugar mixture and about 1 inch away from the bottom of the jar.

Let sit at room temperature, undisturbed, for 1 week.

To remove candies, use a butter knife to puncture the top film, and slowly remove by the stick. If you have trouble removing the candy, gently dip the glass in warm water (not boiling water!) to help loosen the edges. Hang popsicle sticks in another jar with clothespin to dry and harden.

Once dried, store Creeping Crystals in an airtight container in a cool, dry place. They will essentially last forever.

AVATAR DAY UNFRIED DOUGH

Prep Time:
20 minutes (active),
approximately 2 hours (inactive)

Cook Time:
Approximately 15 minutes

Yield: 6 cookies

It's always nice to know you're appreciated, though I'm not sure this no-bake cookie dough would've been my first choice for an Avatar Day food. In recent years, Chin villagers seem to have embraced new versions of unfried dough that aren't quite as sticky, droopy, or loose as the first ones I tried. Nowadays, they hold their shape, and some even have sesame seeds!

—Aang

FOR THE DOUGH:

½ cup coconut oil, melted

2 tablespoons honey

2 cups superfine blanched almond flour

¼ cup desiccated coconut

1 tablespoon toasted white sesame seeds

¼ teaspoon kosher salt

FOR THE DIP:

½ cup mini white chocolate chips

1 cup solid cocoa butter (50 grams)

FOR THE ICING (OPTIONAL):

½ cup powdered sugar

1 to 2 teaspoons whole milk, as needed

1 teaspoon light corn syrup

2 to 3 drops pastel blue food coloring, as needed

TO MAKE THE DOUGH:

In a medium bowl, whisk together coconut oil and honey until well combined. Add almond flour, coconut, sesame seeds, and salt. Mix until a soft dough forms.

Place dough at the center of a half-sheet-tray-sized piece of parchment paper. Cover with another sheet of parchment. Use a rolling pin to roll out the dough to ¼-inch thickness. Remove top sheet of parchment paper.

Use gingerbread-men-shaped cookie cutters to pre-punch the Aang-shaped cookies. Freeze cookie dough until completely firm, about 2 hours.

Repunch cookies with cookie cutter, carefully remove, and place on a sheet tray lined with parchment paper for dipping.

TO MAKE THE DIP:

In a small chocolate tempering pot set over a water bath or steaming water, melt white chocolate and cocoa butter until completely smooth.

Using a cake tester, spear each cookie through the middle, and dip for 1 second in the white chocolate mixture.

Let dangle and dry before setting back down onto parchment-lined sheet tray.

Reserve cookies in freezer for 5 to 10 minutes to be finished with icing.

TO MAKE THE ICING:

Sift powdered sugar into a medium bowl. Add milk and corn syrup, and mix until smooth. Icing should be stiff enough to be piped without spreading too much on the cookie. Add food coloring, and mix until desired color is achieved.

Place icing in a piping bag fitted with a very fine tip. Pipe blue arrows on top of cookies to denote Aang's Air Nation tattoos. Because of the cocoa butter, decorating these cookies is a very forgiving process! If you don't like your icing, you can gently wipe it off with a dry paper towel and start over.

Reserve cookies in the freezer to let icing set up. Cookies can be enjoyed frozen or from the refrigerator!

CABBAGE COOKIES

Prep Time: 6 minutes (active), 45 minutes to 1 hour (inactive)

Cook Time: 33–38 minutes

Yield: 24 cookies

How can my signature dish be anything but perfect? I can guarantee you've never tasted a cookie made this way before—sweet, salty, and utterly full of my precious cabbage. I had to travel to the southern islands of the Earth Kingdom to perfect this technique. Since I've brought it to my bistro, this little treat has become so popular, I've heard even the queens of foreign lands are having their servants make copycat versions to enjoy during teatime. Every day I have new customers requesting these by the box. Soon I'll have made enough money from Cabbage Cookies alone to fund my next big enterprise.

—cabbage merchant

FOR THE COOKIE MIX-INS:

2 tablespoons neutral oil

1 head green cabbage, cored, roughly chopped

2 teaspoons kosher salt

1 teaspoon sugar

2 teaspoons whole fennel seeds

2 teaspoons whole coriander seeds

FOR THE COOKIES:

1 cup unsalted butter, at room temperature

¼ cup sugar

1 teaspoon kosher salt

1 teaspoon baking powder

2 cups all-purpose flour

TO PREPARE THE COOKIE MIX-INS:

Heat oil in a large skillet over high heat until slick and shiny. Add cabbage with salt and sugar. Sauté until cabbage has reduced considerably in size, given up all its moisture, and is deeply charred at edges, 15 to 20 minutes. Transfer cabbage to a food processor, and pulse until finely chopped. Reserve.

Dry-toast the spices in a clean skillet until lightly browned and very fragrant, approximately 3 minutes. Transfer to a spice grinder, and grind coarsely. Reserve.

TO MAKE THE COOKIES:

Cream the butter and sugar in a stand mixer fitted with a paddle attachment on medium speed until fluffy, approximately 3 minutes. Add the salt, baking powder, and the reserved toasted spices. Add the reserved cabbage, and continue to mix until well combined, scraping the edges when necessary.

Add flour in small increments until well combined.

Transfer cookie dough onto two pieces of plastic wrap, and gently roll into a log about 2 inches wide, twisting the ends in opposite directions to seal. Freeze for 45 minutes to 1 hour, or until firm enough to be sliced.

Preheat oven to 350°F. Remove cookie dough from freezer, and slice into ¼-inch-thick cookies. Place cookies on a parchment-lined sheet tray, and bake until golden brown, approximately 15 minutes.

Remove from oven and let cool. Serve warm or at room temperature. Cookies can be stored in an airtight container for up to 3 days at room temperature, or frozen for up to 3 months. Reheat at 350°F before serving.

CACTUS JUICE

Prep Time:
2 minutes (active),
32-48 hours (inactive)

Yield: Serves 1-2

The most quenching drink of them all! Despite what everyone kept saying, *I* didn't feel anything strange when I drank it in the Si Wong desert—it just helps you see and talk to your old friends, that's all. I think if those shops at Misty Palms started bottling this stuff, it'd fly off the shelves! It's so hydrating and even has a tiny bit of sparkle. Team Avatar's loss that they didn't get to try any.

—Sokka

1 Meyer lemon (or any lemon), juiced

1 cup pink or yellow cactus pear juice (from about 8 cactus pears)

½ cup sugar

1 cup hot water

1 tablespoon activated water kefir grains (optional, to add tanginess)

Combine lemon juice, cactus pear juice, sugar, and hot water. Stir to dissolve.

If using water kefir grains, add to the blend once it has cooled to room temperature. Cover with cheesecloth or a coffee filter, and let rest 24 hours at room temperature.

Taste juice for sweetness: If you want it less sweet, let water kefir grains continue to work another 8 to 24 hours.

Strain out water kefir grains, and serve juice chilled or over ice.

KALE SMOOTHIE

Prep Time:
5 minutes

Yield:
Serves 1

Aang is always trying to feed me terrible things like vegetables so I can be "healthy" and an "inspiration to earthbenders everywhere." He tried to serve me this smoothie, but I fed it to Appa when Twinkle Toes wasn't looking. That crazy beast seemed to really enjoy it, so good riddance!

—TOPH

½ cup steamed kale

¼ cup raw walnuts

1 cup coconut water

⅛ teaspoon xanthan gum (optional)

Blend kale, walnuts, and coconut water in blender until smooth. Add xanthan gum for a slightly thicker smoothie, if desired. Serve over ice.

MISTY PALMS MANGO SMOOTHIE

Prep Time:
5 minutes

Yield:
Approximately 1½ cups (12 ounces)

This is still my favorite part of our (very short) Misty Palms experience. Sometimes, Uncle Iroh will make this for me when we don't have the time to visit the desert but still want to enjoy something cool, refreshing, and with a drink umbrella.

—Katara

FOR THE HONEY CARDAMOM SYRUP:

½ cup honey

½ cup water

12 whole green cardamom pods, gently crushed

FOR THE SMOOTHIE BASE:

2 large mangoes, peeled, pitted

¼ cup cold water

Approximately ⅓ cup ice

1 pinch kosher salt

2 tablespoons honey cardamom syrup, from above

¼ teaspoon rosewater

Combine honey with water and green cardamom pods in a small pot over medium heat.

Bring to a light simmer, and let cook 5 minutes on low heat.

Remove from heat and let infuse another 15 minutes.

Strain and reserve in refrigerator.

Combine mangoes with water, ice, salt, syrup, and rosewater in blender.

Blend on high until smooth.

Season with more syrup, salt, or rosewater to taste.

THE JASMINE DRAGON TEA SHOP

The Jasmine Dragon is not just a place but a touchstone of beautiful memories. From Zuko fully recovering upstairs and taking control of his destiny to become a Fire Lord very different from his predecessors to Avatar Aang bringing a new generation of Air Acolytes to meditate inside its very walls, this gentle dragon has seen the Four Nations change and grow into new selves. For me, at this old age I'm just grateful I'm able to retire here. After so many years of war, with unending strife and unease, spending my days soothing others with our tea has been nothing short of a mental, physical, and spiritual balm. It brings me great joy to see my tea bringing travelers from all over the Four Nations together.

Now, remember that brewing tea is much more than just heating up water to make a "hot leaf juice"—it's a thoughtful exercise in appreciating what nature can offer us, our respect for the hard work of others, and a gentle appreciation of being able to take a moment and have some delightful tea. At each step of the process, make sure to really observe and smell your tea leaves, as well as your fresh first, second, and third cup. Feel the warmth of your teapot and teacups in your palms as you ready your tea station. If you'll be rinsing your tea leaves before brewing them, take those moments to reflect upon how you're feeling, how you hope to interact with the tea.

A great joy in tea is that it is a communal practice, and I love sharing tea with others! If you'll be preparing tea for your family and friends, encourage them to also engage with the leaves carefully—even Zuko became a little more grateful to the tea farmers and artisans once he could see the differences in each tea, even though green, oolong, red, and black teas are all from the same plant. Before I discard my used tea leaves, I like to close my eyes and say thank you for offering me this opportunity to have tea in my life.

—Iroh

FRESH GINSENG TEA

Prep Time: 2 minutes

Cook Time: 10-13 minutes

Yield: 1 cup

Now ginseng is an herb all nations can agree on. When made with fresh roots, the infusion is intense yet delicate—a special gift from nature to us. Maybe I'm a bit of a tea-pusher, but a fresh cup of ginseng tea has been my favorite cure-all since I was a young firebender. Now, if only I could get Zuko to like it as much as I do.

As it steeps, the ginseng flavor in your tea will bloom and grow stronger. I recommend you try your tea at 5 minutes to see how you like the taste, and if you prefer more intensity, you can let it keep steeping. Once finished, you can also reuse your ginseng when cooking dinner, like a delicious ginseng and chicken soup!

—Iroh

1 cup hot water

Five ¼-inch-thick quarter-sized coins peeled fresh ginseng

Boil water to 195°F. Place fresh ginseng in tea bag or strainer. Pour water into teacup, and let steep with ginseng for 5 to 8 minutes.

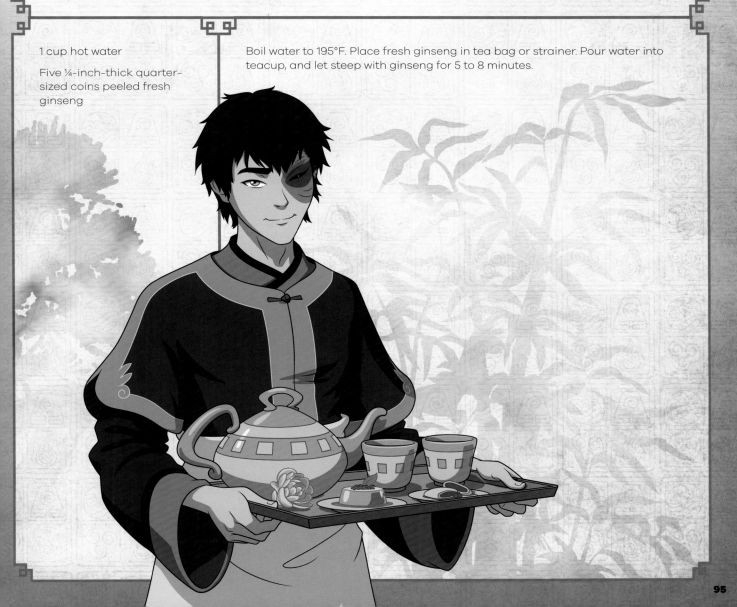

WARMING GINGER TEA

Prep Time: 5 minutes

Cook Time: 7-10 minutes

Yield: Serves 1

There's nothing quite like sipping a cup of hot tea, enjoying some light music, and watching the sunset. This ginger tea is my personal go-to during the cold winter nights in Ba Sing Se, where Zuko and I would stand together and enjoy some people-watching from the second-floor windows of our shop.

—Iroh

1 cup hot water

Five ¼-inch-thick quarter-sized coins peeled fresh ginger

Honey (optional)

Boil water to 195°F. Place fresh ginger in a tea bag or strainer. Pour water into teacup, and let steep with ginger for 5 to 8 minutes. Swirl in some honey if desired.

RED-BLOODED NEPHEW TEA

Prep Time: 2 minutes

Cook Time: 5 minutes

Yield: Serves 1-2

Zuko's favorite blend is bold, complex, and a little confused—just like him, I suppose. I chuckle to myself when I see those who gravitate toward this tea; I know they'll probably get along with my nephew well, having likely also been through a lot at a young age. Zuko is still processing everything he's absorbed all these years, and I know there will be many variations on this tea to come.

—Iroh

1½ cups hot water

2 teaspoons cinnamon shavings (from about 1 cinnamon stick)

1 piece candied ginger

3 dried jujubes

10 goji berries

1½ teaspoons pu-erh tea

1½ teaspoons Lapsang souchong

1 lemon or orange peel

3 whole cloves

Boil water to 195°F. Place cinnamon, ginger, jujubes, goji, and tea leaves into a teapot. Pour water into teapot, and let steep 3 minutes. Portion into 1 or 2 teacups.

Stud lemon or orange peel with cloves. Light cloves on fire, then drop into teacup. Serve!

LYCHEE JUICE

Prep Time:
5 minutes

Yield:
Serves 4

In the thick of summer, lychee juice is the most popular drink on the shop's menu. Made in the same manner as at the cantinas at Misty Palms, this is a treat that will instantly refresh you. Plus, it has the added bonus that it's easy enough even Zuko can make it.

—Iroh

One 20-ounce can lychees in syrup, drained and rinsed

¾ cup cold water

¼ cup ice (3 ounces)

1 pinch kosher salt

2 to 4 slices Meyer lemon (or any lemon, optional)

Combine lychees with water, ice, and salt in blender. Blend on high until smooth. Serve with slices of Meyer lemon, if desired.

CUCUMBER ALOE JUICE

Prep Time:
2 minutes

Yield:
Serves 2

This thirst-quenching beverage started as a particular request from my sandbender friends, but it is now a regular on the menu for everyone in the Earth Nation to enjoy. It's cooling, just sweet enough, and has a slight vegetable taste from the cucumber.

—Iroh

½ cup unsweetened aloe juice

⅓ cup cucumber juice

1 tablespoon sugar

Combine all ingredients and stir to combine. Serve chilled.

JASMINE GREEN TEA

Achieving balance in this tea is what makes it really shine. By bringing together different expressions of jasmine—as fragrant flowers, also naturally infused into rolled green tea leaves—this tea maintains its gentle nature while being strong enough to stand alone and stand out. After all, there is a reason I named my shop after it! It is a reminder of the very nature of life: Where there is balance, there is peace.

—Iroh

¾ cup hot water

1 teaspoon dried jasmine flowers

½ teaspoon Japanese sencha

2 rolled jasmine pearls

Boil water to 180°F. Place jasmine flowers, sencha, and jasmine pearls into a small teapot. Pour water into teapot, and let steep 3 minutes. If drinking the first steep, serve immediately. If not, discard and add fresh hot water. Let steep 3 minutes, then serve immediately.

JASMINE GREEN TEA KOMBUCHA

Prep Time: 5 minutes
Cook Time:
12-15 minutes (active),
5-10 days (inactive)
Yield: 8-10 cups

After enough requests for a cold version of my jasmine blend, I began to experiment with new flavors, as cool beverages need more seasoning to harmonize the ingredients. I settled on a fiery, bright addition of ginger and just a light sparkle to keep our customers' tongues abuzz.

—Iroh

2 tablespoons dried jasmine flowers

1 tablespoon Japanese sencha

10 rolled jasmine pearls

6 cups hot water

Sugar

¼ cup peeled, chopped fresh ginger

1 SCOBY
(symbiotic culture of bacteria and yeast, available online in convenient starter kits)

To set yourself up for success, it is important to sterilize your equipment before embarking on your fermentation journey. Rinse all of your tools and containers thoroughly with distilled white vinegar or with boiling water for approximately 10 minutes. If boiling, allow all equipment to cool before using, as heat can kill the good bacteria in the SCOBY and kombucha.

Combine jasmine flowers, sencha, and jasmine pearls in a large bowl or pot.

Heat 2 cups of water to 180°F. Pour over jasmine mix, and steep 3 minutes. Strain into a medium pot.

Heat another 2 cups of water to 180°F. Pour over jasmine mix, and steep 3 minutes. Strain into same pot.

Heat the remaining 2 cups of water to 180°F. Pour over jasmine mix, and steep 3 minutes. Strain into same pot. Discard jasmine mix.

Measure your final cups of tea. The rule of thumb for calculating the necessary amount of sugar is 1 cup of suger per 1 gallon of tea.

Divide tea between kombucha fermentation vessel (two-thirds of tea) and pot (one-third of tea).

Add sugar to pot, and heat gently until dissolved. Pour into fermentation vessel.

Let sweetened tea cool below 140°F to ensure the heat does not kill the SCOBY.

Plop SCOBY into fermentation vessel.

Cover the top of the fermentation vessel with a breathable cloth or cheesecloth, and secure with rubber band.

Let ferment 5 to 10 days in a warm (80°F), clean environment. At 3 days, start tasting your kombucha to determine when you want to stop the fermentation, depending on your desired sugar level. At this point, you can also add the ginger.

If you want your kombucha to be fizzy, bottle the kombucha in swing-top bottles before all the sugar has been eaten by the SCOBY and the kombucha is no longer sweet. Be careful when opening them!

Store finished kombucha in the refrigerator, and consume within 7 days for optimal freshness.

If your SCOBY develops any off-color molds during the fermentation process, discard the entire batch of kombucha and start over.

APPA BLEND BUBBLE TEA

Prep Time: 10 minutes

Cook Time:
30 minutes (active),
30 minutes (inactive)

Yield: Serves 4

Zuko and Aang might not have liked my first few experiments with bubble tea, but let's not fixate on that. It's been a hit since then! My customers love these chewy tapioca balls so much, I've started adding them to all sorts of teas at the shop. The top seller, though, is always this particular combination of rich, malty black teas from the mountainous eastern slopes of the Earth Nation.

—Iroh

FOR THE BOBA:

¼ cup tapioca flour, plus more for dusting

⅛ cup boiling water (25 grams)

FOR THE SYRUP:

½ cup light brown sugar

3 cups water

FOR THE TEA:

2 tablespoons Chinese black tea, preferably Qimen (or English breakfast or other black tea)

2 cups boiling water

Milk of choice

TO MAKE THE BOBA:

Place tapioca flour in a small bowl. Drizzle with boiling water while mixing with a fork.

Transfer mixture to a surface lightly dusted with tapioca flour, and knead with hands until the dough is smooth.

Form dough into a long rope ¼-inch thick, and cut into small pieces ⅛-inch thick.

Roll each piece into a ball. Reserve in freezer if not moving to the next step immediately.

TO MAKE THE SYRUP:

Combine sugar and water in a medium pot over medium-high heat, and bring to a light boil.

Once sugar has melted completely, add boba, and bring back to a light boil. Continue to cook until the balls turn completely translucent, approximately 20 minutes.

Let cool, and reserve boba in syrup, in refrigerator.

TO MAKE THE TEA:

Steep tea in water for 5 minutes, then strain. Chill tea in refrigerator until cold.

When ready to serve, place boba at the base of each glass. Add ½ cup to ¾ cup chilled tea. Add milk of choice, to desired amount. Serve!

TEA LEAF JUICE

Prep Time: 2 minutes

**Cook Time:
5 minutes (active), 30 minutes
(inactive, if serving chilled)**

Yield: 1 cup

The Jasmine Dragon wouldn't feel right without a few tastes of home. Now that the nations are united, even the elites of Ba Sing Se like to sip on this frothy concoction originally hailing from the Fire Nation. Of course, I couldn't let my customers have *all* the fun; that's why I nicknamed this drink "tea leaf juice"—for the fact you're actually eating tea leaves—so I can tease Zuko into adulthood.

—Iroh

¾ teaspoon matcha powder

1 cup 190°F water

Ice cubes (optional, if serving cold)

Carefully sift matcha powder into a medium bowl.

Add half of hot water, and carefully whisk to combine with matcha using chasen bamboo whisk.

Add rest of water, and continue to whisk until very frothy and smooth. *For extra froth, you can also use a milk frother at this step.*

Serve hot as is, or chill in refrigerator until cold, and serve over ice cubes.

BENDER TEA

Prep time: 2 minutes

**Cook Time:
10 minutes (active), 18-20
minutes (inactive)**

Yield: At least 2 cups

I named this blend after Aang and Katara, as their harmonious ways of bending began a new era of deeper understanding and cross-cultural exchange among all benders. This tea reflects their beautiful legacy: It grows atop the mountains of the southern islands, its flavor influenced by the region's independent spirit and the mysterious fog created by water and air.

—Iroh

3 tablespoons Taiwanese oolong tea, preferably from Dong Ding (6 grams)

¼ cup boiling water

1 cup boiling water

1 cup boiling water

Additional boiling water, if desired

Warm teapot using hot water, if desired. Pour out all excess water.

Put tea leaves into teapot. Pour ¼ cup boiling water over tea leaves and let sit 15 seconds to rinse. Strain and discard water.

Pour 1 cup boiling water over tea leaves, and let steep 1 to 2 minutes. Pour tea into teacups and enjoy.

Pour another 1 cup boiling water over tea leaves, and let steep 2 minutes. Pour tea into teacups and enjoy.

Repeat with fresh boiling water for as many times as desired.

FIRE NATION

If it's not spicy, it's not from the Fire Nation. I'm so tired of Earth Kingdom food always being mistaken as Fire Nation grub—they aren't the same, you know, even if there's some crossover from the colonies.

While the Fire Nation isn't as big as the Earth Kingdom, our region is too vast to be described in just a few sentences. Sample your way around the Capital, and you'll be treated to all sorts of recipes that have been carefully honed through time and practice for centuries. Nothing is too small or too insignificant to be without a rule book when it comes to making the absolute best for the Fire Lord. At any old food stand, you'll find a cook who has been carefully perfecting their signature dish for generations.

Much of Fire Nation food is based on control and respect for firebending. Bending coals just hot enough to toast the outsides of a sizzle-crisp but not set it alight is not just a demonstration of skill but also a way to show your appreciation for and connection to our nation itself. That's why the chiles of Fire Nation food are so important—eating them helps bring out our firebending talents, and nurturing the special Fire Nation chile plants is a revered practice.

Some of my favorite dishes across the Fire Nation have to be sweets and drinks, though. You'd be surprised how excellent sugar and spice work together, especially at the end of a really good dinner.

—Zuko

FLAMING FIRE FLAKES

Prep Time: 5 minutes

Cook Time: 7 hours, 25 minutes

Yield: Serves 3-4

I never learned to breathe fire like my uncle Iroh, so eating extra-spicy fire flakes and exhaling a mouthful of smoke is the closest I'm going to get. Every year there are competitions to rate the best fire flakes. I think it's hard to tell, as they're so common now and have so many variations—some even come packaged in puffy bags that never go stale! I guess if I had to pick, the special shrimp ones from the palace kitchens still rank number-one in my mind.

—Zuko

Flameo, hotman!

—Aang

FOR THE SHRIMP STOCK:

1 tablespoon neutral oil

½ medium yellow onion, sliced

5 cloves garlic, sliced

1-inch knob fresh ginger, peeled and sliced

4 bird's-eye chiles, stemmed and chopped

3 cups shrimp of any variety, head on, shells on (350 grams)

2 teaspoons red pepper flakes

3 cups water

Kosher salt

Sugar

Ground white pepper

FOR THE FIRE FLAKES:

¼ cup mini tapioca pearls

Neutral oil, for frying

1 tablespoon togarashi

1 tablespoon ground Sansho pepper

1 tablespoon ground red pepper flakes

TO MAKE THE SHRIMP STOCK:

Heat the oil in a medium pot over medium until slick and shiny. Add the onion, garlic, ginger, and chiles, and sauté until onions are translucent, 3 to 5 minutes. Add shrimp, and sauté another 2 minutes. Add red pepper flakes and water, then bring to a light simmer. Season with salt, sugar, and white pepper to taste. Let simmer, covered, 1 hour. Remove from heat and strain. Reserve liquid.

TO MAKE THE FIRE FLAKES:

Combine 2 cups of the reserved shrimp stock with the tapioca pearls in a small pot over medium heat. Bring to a light simmer, then cover and let cook until tapioca pearls are clear and fully swelled, and the liquid has taken on a jelly-like consistency.

Transfer mixture to a silicone mat or piece of parchment paper, and spread it into one thin, even layer.

Dehydrate mixture in a dehydrator at 140°F until completely dry and the chip snaps easily, approximately 6 hours. If you don't have a dehydrator, set your oven to the lowest temperature it will go, turn on the fan, and dehydrate in the oven until dry. Reserve the fire flake base in an airtight container at room temperature until you are ready to fry.

Heat 1 to 2 inches of oil in a medium high-walled pot to 375°F. Break fire flake base into quarter-sized pieces. Fry chips in oil until they puff up, approximately 30 seconds. Do this in batches to keep the oil at the right temperature.

Drain fire flakes on paper towels, and immediately toss with togarashi, Sansho, and ground chile. Serve immediately.

SIZZLE-CRISPS

Prep Time:
2 minutes (active),
1 hour (inactive)
Cook Time: 10-15 minutes
Yield: 12-14 sizzle-crisps

Sizzle-crisps have been my favorite afternoon snack since my childhood. Everyone has their favorite street vendor, each with wilder and wilder tales of how *their* version is somehow spicier than the next. I'm not the trendy type, so I stick with the classic—peppery, but nothing at the level of those now nicknamed Dragon's Breath after my uncle.

—Zuko

2 tablespoons chile oil

2 teaspoons Sansho pepper powder

2 teaspoons togarashi

¼ teaspoon garlic powder

1 teaspoon sugar (optional)

One 12-ounce package sliced bacon, preferably applewood smoked, cut into thirds

Combine all ingredients in a medium bowl, and thoroughly coat each slice of bacon. Let marinate at least 1 hour.

Preheat oven to 325°F. Place bacon strips on a sheet tray outfitted with a wire rack.

Roast until bacon has shrunk considerably in size, is curling at edges, and lightly blackened at sides, 10 to 15 minutes. You'll want it to be almost burned, this is a Fire Nation snack after all!

Remove bacon from oven, and drain on paper towels before serving.

Don't waste the bacon fat! Strain it and use it for other tasty foods like a bacony chile sauce for noodles.

KOMODO CHICKEN

Prep Time:
2 minutes (active),
8-12 hours (inactive)

Cook Time: 1 hour 15 minutes

Yield: Serves 2

I'll never forget the cold Komodo chicken Zuko brought me when I was locked away in the Capital City prison. I almost didn't eat it after he left, my heart was so broken. Tasting those soggy tenders reminded me of simpler times, when Zuko and I would sneak into the palace's kitchen and watch them fry up batches of chicken in glimmering oil pots. We would gobble as many pieces as we could reach before the chefs chased us away. Even in the hurry, I always managed to stuff a few in my pockets to delight Zuko afterward.

—Iroh

FOR THE SPICY HONEY:

4 cloves garlic

½ cup honey

2 teaspoons red pepper flakes

FOR THE FRIED CHICKEN:

2 boneless, skinless chicken thighs, sliced into 1-inch strips

1 tablespoon high quality sake

2 tablespoons soy sauce

1 red jalapeño, minced

2 cloves garlic, minced

2 teaspoons chile oil

Potato starch, for dredging

Neutral oil, for frying

TO MAKE THE SPICY HONEY:

Combine garlic, honey, and red pepper flakes in a small pot over medium heat. Bring to a very gentle simmer, then lower heat to the lowest level possible for 1 hour, allowing the mixture to infuse.

Transfer mixture to a small container, and let infuse in refrigerator 8 hours or overnight. Once infused, strain and let cool to room temperature. Store in refrigerator.

TO MAKE THE FRIED CHICKEN:

In a medium bowl, combine chicken with sake, soy sauce, jalapeño, garlic, and chile oil, and mix thoroughly. Let marinate 8 hours or overnight.

Dredge chicken in potato starch, dusting off any excess.

In a deep, heavy-bottomed frying pan over medium-high heat, bring 1 to 2 inches of oil to 340°F, then fry chicken in batches until golden brown. Maintain the oil temperature at around 325°F. Drain fried chicken on paper towels.

Heat oil to 400°F, then fry chicken a second time in batches until a deep golden brown. Maintain the oil temperature around 375°F. Drain fried chicken on paper towels.

Serve with spicy honey.

FRESH JIANG HUI CLAMS

Prep Time: 10 minutes

Cook Time: 7-11 minutes

Yield: Serves 3-4

A few years after we left Jang Hui, Team Avatar sat down for dinner at a nice restaurant in the Fire Nation capital and were told we came just in time for a special harvest of Jang Hui clams. Can you imagine? In such a short time, what was once such a polluted place had become famous for its seafood, which our server told us were "exceptionally plump, with hints of wakame brine and ocean kumquat." Eating those clams was a satisfying reminder that nothing is so far gone it can't be brought back into balance again.

—Katara

1 tablespoon neutral oil

2 teaspoons chili oil

½ medium onion, peeled, sliced

5 cloves garlic (18 grams)

3 bird's eye chilies (8 grams)

1-inch knob fresh ginger, peeled and sliced (12 grams)

1 teaspoon kosher salt

2 pounds manila clams, cleaned and purged

½ cup sake (40 grams)

Togarashi, as desired

1 scallion, sliced thinly on bias

1 lemon, cut into wedges

Heat oil in a medium pot over medium heat until slick and shiny.

Add onion, garlic, chilies, and ginger with salt. Sauté 2 to 3 minutes until onions are lightly translucent.

Add clams and continue to sauté 2 to 3 minutes.

Add sake. Cover the pot and reduce heat to medium-low.

Cook clams in pot 3 to 5 minutes, checking intermittently to see how many clams have opened up.

Once clams have all opened up, remove from heat.

Garnish with togarashi, scallion, and lemon wedges.

ROKU-STYLE FLAMING HOT CHICKEN SKEWERS

Prep Time:
5 minutes (active),
30 minutes (inactive)

Cook Time: 16 minutes

Yield: Serves 4

Sokka ate his fair share of "meat on sticks," as he likes to call it, when Team Avatar showed up on the eastern Fire Nation shores and pretended to be Fire nationals. I'll bet he missed the best kind though—you have to ask for "Roku style" for the vendors to add the spicy oil and scallions from the secret menu.

—Zuko

4 boneless, skinless chicken thighs, cut into 2-inch pieces

Kosher salt

Fresh ground black pepper

2 red bird's eye chiles, minced

2 tablespoons mirin

2 tablespoons chile oil

4 to 6 scallions, whites only, cut into 2-inch pieces

In a large bowl, liberally salt and pepper chicken thigh pieces. Add chiles, mirin, and chili oil. Toss to combine, and let marinate 30 minutes.

Skewer chicken thighs and scallion whites, alternating between the two, onto metal skewers or wet wooden skewers.

If using a yakitori grill, set up the grill according to the manufacturer's instructions, then grill the chicken skewers until the internal temperature reaches at least 165°F.

If using an oven, set your broiler to high. Place your oven rack on the uppermost position, and place the skewers on a sheet tray lined with aluminum foil. Broil skewers until well browned on one side, then flip and brown the other side, approximately 3 minutes each side. Turn off broiler, heat the oven to 400°F, and place the skewers in the middle rack of the oven. Roast until the internal temperature reaches at least 165°F, approximately 10 minutes.

FIRE NOODLES

If you need a spicy pick-me-up, I'd recommend a bowl of spicy noodles. These curly noodles are so hot, they'll get you right up out of your seat and ready to take on the world. I especially like eating them for breakfast, sometimes with an onsen egg if I've had the time for a warm dip.

—Zuko

FOR THE CHILE OIL:

8 dried red chiles

1 tablespoon whole Sansho pepper (or substitute green Sichuan peppercorns)

2 teaspoons black peppercorns

2-inch knob fresh ginger, peeled and minced

2 teaspoons wasabi paste

½ teaspoon garlic powder

1 teaspoon shiitake powder (optional)

½ teaspoon kosher salt

½ teaspoon sugar

1 cup neutral oil

FOR THE SPICY BROTH:

2 tablespoons neutral oil

½ medium yellow onion, sliced

6 cloves garlic, sliced

10 shiitake mushroom caps, chopped

2-inch knob fresh ginger, peeled and sliced

4 jalapeños, stemmed and chopped

3 tablespoons red miso

2 pounds pork neck bone

TO MAKE THE CHILE OIL:

Preheat oven to 400°F. Toast chiles on a sheet tray 1 to 2 minutes, until darkened but not black. Remove and let cool completely. Pulverize into powder with a spice grinder. Dry-toast Sansho and black pepper in a small skillet over medium heat until lightly fragrant, 2 to 3 minutes. Let cool completely, and grind coarsely with a spice grinder.

Combine chiles with Sansho, black pepper, ginger, wasabi, garlic, shiitake powder, salt, and sugar in a heatproof container. Heat the oil in a small pot until it reaches 300°F. Carefully pour oil over chile mixture. It will bubble and steam immensely. Stir to combine, and let cool completely. Let chile oil infuse in the refrigerator overnight before serving.

TO MAKE THE SPICY BROTH:

In a large pot, heat oil over medium heat until slick and shiny. Add onion, garlic, mushrooms, ginger, and jalapeño, and cook until onions are translucent, 5 to 8 minutes. Add red miso, and mix until well combined. Add pork neck bone and anchovy.

Deglaze with mirin, and cook until mirin has evaporated. Add water with salt and black pepper. Bring mixture to a very light boil, skimming the surface. Bring mixture to a medium boil. Cover and let cook 8 hours or overnight.

Strain broth. The yield should be 2 quarts, or 8 cups.

CONTINUED ON NEXT PAGE

1 tablespoon dried anchovy (optional)

¼ cup mirin

1½ gallons water

1 teaspoon kosher salt

1 teaspoon fresh ground black pepper

FOR ASSEMBLY:

1 tablespoon neutral oil

½ medium size yellow onion, minced

4 cloves garlic, minced

1-inch knob fresh ginger, peeled and minced

2 jalapeños, stemmed, minced

One 3½-ounce package beech mushrooms, separated into individual mushrooms (optional)

½ pound ground pork

1 tablespoon soy sauce

1 tablespoon mirin

Kosher salt, to taste

4 packages ramen noodles, cooked per package instructions

Spicy chile oil, for garnish

Sliced scallions, for garnish

TO ASSEMBLE THE SOUP:

In a medium pot, heat oil over medium until slick and shiny. Add onion, garlic, ginger, and jalapeños, and sauté 2 to 3 minutes or until onions are translucent. Add mushrooms, and continue to cook 2 to 3 minutes until they let out their water. Add ground pork, soy sauce, and mirin, breaking up the pieces with a spatula. Cook another 2 to 3 minutes. Add 2 quarts of the spicy broth, and bring to a light simmer. Continue until ground pork is completely cooked through. Season with salt to taste.

Arrange ramen in bowls and top with broth. Garnish with spicy chile oil and scallions.

THE FIREBENDING MASTERS

Prep Time:
5 minutes

Yield:
Serves 2

The Sun Warriors gifted me and Aang so much about firebending that I never learned in Fire Nation school, and I hope to honor their traditions by teaching their philosophy and methods to the next generation. Like my uncle, I promised to never reveal their location or who they are, but that doesn't mean their knowledge will be lost after I step down from the throne. Their forms of firebending movements like the Dancing Dragon are now mandatory in schools, and their calm yet fiery demeanor taught as the precursor to anyone learning to firebend. It was my uncle that nicknamed this drink, a soothing and spicy cleansing tonic to set your mind at ease for firebending practice.

—Zuko

1 tablespoon unsweetened tamarind pulp

1 bird's eye chili, stemmed, seeded, minced

1 cup pineapple juice (preferably freshly juiced)

1 tablespoon agave nectar

1 cup plain sparkling water

6 ice cubes

1 bird's eye chili, halved lengthwise, for garnish

Mix together tamarind, chili, pineapple juice, and agave until well combined.

Divide mixture between 2 glasses with 3 ice cubes each.

Top each drink with sparkling water.

Garnish with chili, if desired.

AZULA'S LIGHTNING

Prep Time:
5 minutes (active),
1-3 days (inactive)

Yield: Serves 2

I was appalled when I first heard this drink was going to bear my name. How can something so static like a beverage even attempt to convey the sense of power I possess? Mai eventually convinced me to try it—only she ever dares bother me with suggestions I've already refused—and . . . it's not terrible. If the people of the Fire Nation see me in this way, like a jolt of lightning, cold and hot at the same time, I suppose that's not such a bad thing.

—Azula

2 Asian pears of any variety, peeled, cored, and juiced

2 teaspoons lemon juice

1 Persian cucumber, juiced

¼ teaspoon kosher salt

Sugar

2 bird's-eye chiles or serrano chiles, stemmed and sliced

1 drop blue food coloring

In a glass jar, combine pear juice, lemon juice, cucumber juice, salt, and sugar to taste. Add peppers, and let infuse in the refrigerator 1 to 3 days or until desired level of spice is achieved. Strain out peppers. Add blue food coloring, and serve chilled.

EMBER ISLAND CHERRY ICE CREAM

Prep Time:
2 minutes (active),
2 hours (inactive)

Cook Time:
30-35 minutes

Yield: Serves 6

Zuko knows this is my favorite flavor of the offerings at the Ember Island ice-cream shop, all the other ones are *terribly* boring. The fact that Azula hates it after her little cherry-pit incident makes it all the better, honestly. If Ember Island wasn't so annoying to get to, I'd come here all the time just for a cone. It's a real mystery to me why they don't sell it in the Capital, too. Maybe I should bring that up with my father, not that he's ever of any use.

—Mai

1⅓ cups cherry puree
(430 grams)

2 bird's eye chilies,
stemmed, minced (6 grams)

½ cup white sugar
(110 grams)

½ teaspoon kosher salt

1⅓ cups heavy cream
(300 grams)

1 teaspoon gochugaru
(Korean red chili flake)

Combine cherry puree, bird's eye chilies, sugar, salt, heavy cream, and gochugaru in a small pot, and bring to a very light simmer to ensure salt and sugar have melted.

Transfer to food-safe container and place in refrigerator until completely chilled, at least 2 hours.

Process ice cream base in an ice cream maker based on manufacturer's recommendations. (On Ember Island, the machines are filled with big rock salt and churned by hand!) If you don't have an ice cream maker, there are several alternative ways to churn the base by hand, such as using a hand mixer or food processor, but an ice cream maker will yield the best results.

FIRE GUMMIES

Prep Time:
15 minutes (active),
2 hours 5 minutes (inactive)
Cook Time: 5-10 minutes
Yield: 8-12 fire gummies

Fire gummies are a local specialty on Ember Island. And while they're available year-round, I like to eat them by the handful during the winter months. It's a sight most tourists never see: the island cloaked in snow, with only a few household fires luminous in the distance. I like to wander the streets to clear my head, with a cup of gummies—always strawberry flavor, like you'd find at the shops back in the Capital—to heat me up from the inside, the tunes of the Ember Island Theater still tinkling in my mind.

—Iroh

FOR THE CENTERS:

Approximately 1 cup strawberries, stemmed

3 red jalapeños, stemmed

1 cup water

¼ teaspoon kosher salt

⅓ to ½ cup white sugar, to taste

Unflavored gelatin powder

FOR THE MOCHI:

1 cup glutinous rice flour

¾ cup water

¼ cup sugar

Cornstarch, for dusting

SPECIAL SUPPLIES:

Semi-sphere mochi or candy mold

TO PREPARE THE CENTERS:

Combine strawberries, jalapeños, water, and salt in blender. Puree until very smooth. Add sugar to taste.

Strain mixture through fine-mesh strainer into a medium-to-large bowl.

For every 1 cup of strained liquid, whisk in 4 packets (or 3 tablespoons) of gelatin. Let bloom for 5 minutes.

Transfer bloomed mixture to a small pot, and gently heat on low until gelatin has completely dissolved and temperature has reached at least 125°F to activate the gelatin. If you don't have a thermometer, you can bring it to a boil.

Spoon 1 teaspoon of strawberry mixture into each semi-sphere in the mochi or candy mold.

Freeze until completely solid, approximately 2 hours. Remove from molds, and reserve for wrapping.

TO PREPARE THE MOCHI:

In a microwave-safe bowl, whisk together rice flour, water, and sugar until smooth.

Microwave for 1 minute. Remove, stir, and place back into microwave.

Continue to microwave at 30-second intervals until the mochi is sticky, semi-translucent, and has no "raw dough" taste.

Working quickly, transfer mochi dough to cutting board dusted generously with cornstarch.

Roll dough in cornstarch, then roll out dough to ⅛-inch thickness.

Use a ring cutter to cut circles twice the diameter of the bottoms of the gummy centers.

Pick up a disc of mochi dough. Using a brush, dust off cornstarch from the side of the mochi facing you, and place one gummy center at the center, flat side facing you.

Fold together all the mochi dough at the base of the gummy center (the flat side) and pinch together to seal. Repeat with all dough and centers, and serve. Mochi can be stored at room temperature for up to 5 days.

125

INDEX

INSIGHT
EDITIONS

PO Box 3088
San Rafael, CA 94912

www.insighteditions.com

Find us on Facebook: www.facebook.com/InsightEditions
Follow us on Twitter: @insighteditions

Library of Congress Cataloging-in-Publication Data available.

ISBN: 978-1-64722-338-0

Publisher: Raoul Goff
VP of Licensing and Partnerships: Vanessa Lopez
VP of Creative: Chrissy Kwasnik
VP of Manufacturing: Alix Nicholaeff
Editorial Director: Vicki Jaeger
Designer: Brooke McCullum
Editor: Maya Alpert
Editorial Assistant: Elizabeth Ovieda
Senior Production Editor: Jennifer Bentham
Production Manager: Sam Taylor
Senior Production Manager, Subsidiary Rights: Lina s Palma

Nickelodeon
Senior Editor: Raina Moore
Associate Art Director: Susan Choi

ROOTS of PEACE   REPLANTED PAPER

Insight Editions, in association with Roots of Peace, will plant two trees for each tree used in the manufacturing of this book. Roots of Peace is an internationally renowned humanitarian organization dedicated to eradicating land mines worldwide and converting war-torn lands into productive farms and wildlife habitats. Roots of Peace will plant two million fruit and nut trees in Afghanistan and provide farmers there with the skills and support necessary for sustainable land use.

Manufactured in China by Insight Editions

10 9 8 7 6